P9-ARY-084

New Directions for
Community Colleges

Arthur M. Cohen
EDITOR-IN-CHIEF

Caroline Q. Durdella
Nathan R. Durdella
ASSOCIATE EDITORS

Applying the College Completion Agenda to Practice

Katherine L. Hughes
Andrea Venezia

EDITORS

Number 167 • Fall 2014
Jossey-Bass
San Francisco

APPLYING THE COLLEGE COMPLETION AGENDA TO PRACTICE
Katherine L. Hughes, Andrea Venezia (eds.)
New Directions for Community Colleges, no. 167

Arthur M. Cohen, Editor-in-Chief
Caroline Q. Durdella, Nathan R. Durdella, Associate Editors

NEW DIRECTIONS FOR COMMUNITY COLLEGES (ISSN 0194-3081, electronic ISSN 1536-0733) is part of The Jossey-Bass Higher and Adult Education Series and is published quarterly by Wiley Subscription Services, Inc., A Wiley Company, at Jossey-Bass, One Montgomery St., Ste. 1200, San Francisco, CA 94104. POSTMASTER: Send address changes to New Directions for Community Colleges, Jossey-Bass, One Montgomery St., Ste. 1200, San Francisco, CA 94104.

SUBSCRIPTIONS cost $89 for individuals in the U.S., Canada, and Mexico, and $113 in the rest of the world for print only; $89 in all regions for electronic only; $98 in the U.S., Canada, and Mexico for combined print and electronic; $122 for combined print and electronic in the rest of the world. Institutional print only subscriptions are $311 in the U.S., $351 in Canada and Mexico, and $385 in the rest of the world; electronic only subscriptions are $311 in all regions; combined print and electronic subscriptions are $357 in the U.S., $397 in Canada and Mexico, and $431 in the rest of the world.

EDITORIAL CORRESPONDENCE should be sent to the Editor-in-Chief, Arthur M. Cohen, at 1749 Mandeville Lane, Los Angeles, CA 90049. All manuscripts receive anonymous reviews by external referees.

New Directions for Community Colleges is indexed in CIJE: Current Index to Journals in Education (ERIC), Contents Pages in Education (T&F), Current Abstracts (EBSCO), Ed/Net (Simpson Communications), Education Index/Abstracts (H. W. Wilson), Educational Research Abstracts Online (T&F), ERIC Database (Education Resources Information Center), and Resources in Education (ERIC).

Microfilm copies of issues and articles are available in 16mm and 35mm, as well as microfiche in 105mm, through University Microfilms Inc., 300 North Zeeb Road, Ann Arbor, MI 48106-1346.

CONTENTS

EDITORS' NOTES

Significant pressure is on community colleges—and all higher education institutions—to increase student completion rates. As the ability to track students' progress through college has improved, the inability to effectively support many—and in some cases most—students through to graduation has become of national concern. Multistate initiatives such as Achieving the Dream, Completion by Design, the Developmental Education Initiative, and Complete College America, along with math reform efforts such as Statway, Quantway, and the New Mathways, have emerged and built upon one another in driving change grounded in evidence. Pressure from the Obama administration, philanthropic foundations, industry representatives, state policymakers, and others has spurred a sharp focus on the kinds of supports, incentives, and programmatic changes necessary to help a larger proportion of students succeed. This all comes after years of budget-cutting at the federal, state, and local levels, along with ongoing demographic changes that, when combined, are forcing postsecondary education systems and institutions to do more with less for an often increasingly underprepared entering student body.

The Winter 2013 volume of *New Directions for Community Colleges*, titled *The College Completion Agenda: Practical Approaches for Reaching the Big Goal* (Phillips & Horowitz, 2013), presented informative articles addressing reforms of different aspects of community colleges, such as the role of leadership in transforming institutional culture, using data to drive change, redesigning academic pathways to better encourage student persistence and completion, and the importance of financial aid, among other topics. These, together, illustrate that the field has made significant progress in developing the knowledge and strategies needed to increase credential completion.

This volume builds on that work in providing a set of chapters that elucidate the change processes underway in institutions and classrooms. The following chapters, mostly authored or coauthored by practitioners, describe the catalysts, the efforts, the false starts and mistakes, and the successes achieved. The aim is to add to the growing body of literature on evidence-based change in a way that helps practitioners understand clearly how these innovations were developed, implemented, and scaled, so as to apply lessons regarding replication in different contexts and under different conditions. Overburdened and resource-strapped community college educators need not reinvent reform strategies but can learn from those already initiated and in place.

New Directions for Community Colleges, no. 167, Fall 2014 © 2014 Wiley Periodicals, Inc.
Published online in Wiley Online Library (wileyonlinelibrary.com) • DOI: 10.1002/cc.20105

As developmental education has been receiving intensive scrutiny as of late, the volume includes three chapters describing new approaches that are showing improved student outcomes. Susan Bickerstaff, Maria Scott Cormier, and Di Xu, from the Community College Research Center, and Barbara Lontz, from Montgomery County Community College in Pennsylvania, present a case study of an arithmetic and prealgebra course redesign, *Concepts of Numbers*, that adopts a new instructional approach. Next, Peter Adams and Donna McKusick, of the Community College of Baltimore County, reflect on the development and growth of the Accelerated Learning Program (ALP), the college's developmental writing program. Both chapters emphasize how course instructors needed significant support in teaching differently. And both courses are now being replicated in other institutions.

Furthering the theme of scaling and spread of reform, the third chapter addressing developmental education, by Katie Hern with Myra Snell, tells a compelling tale of data-driven change through a community of practice across multiple colleges in California. These authors express clearly the many forces working against change—entrenched beliefs about students' capabilities, lack of curricula and textbooks for reimagined courses, inflexible transfer articulation policies, and lack of policy support generally—that perseverance and presentation of evidence are breaking down, little by little.

The next two chapters focus on new approaches to supporting students as they adjust to college, select courses and majors, and strive in the classroom. Mina Dadgar, Thad Nodine, Kathy Reeves Bracco, and Andrea Venezia argue for a better integration of institutions' instruction and support services aspects and provide concrete examples from the field. They and others have pointed out the fact that community college students generally need far more support than the colleges' resources allow, so building guidance and assistance into courses can be efficient as well as more effective than the status quo. Gary Rodwell outlines how an online navigation system can empower students to understand where they are in the "progression continuum" at their colleges and what lies ahead if they are to graduate. This, then, enables them to plan and make rational choices connected to their education goals.

In the following chapter, Lenore Rodicio and Susan Mayer, of Miami Dade College, and Davis Jenkins, from the Community College Research Center, write of how the college has taken these ideas to full scale, with a college-wide overhaul of how entering students are advised and continuously guided through their programs. This has necessitated investing in additional advising staff, deeper involvement of faculty in student support, and a mapping of clear, structured program pathways to help in student decision making and more efficient completion. The result has been, as the authors characterize it, truly transformative change.

Large-scale change is also underway in North Carolina, as R. Edward Bowling, Sharon Morrissey, and George M. Fouts, all community college practitioners, describe in their chapter. Through the community colleges'

NEW DIRECTIONS FOR COMMUNITY COLLEGES • DOI: 10.1002/cc

involvement in Completion by Design (CBD), policy and practice changes are occurring within individual colleges, while state policy is evolving through a parallel process to support the scaling of those efforts statewide. While the colleges worked to develop clear, prescriptive pathways for students aligned with workforce needs, the State Advisory Board for the initiative (composed of postsecondary and K–12 leaders from across the state) developed a list of policy implications based on the colleges' work for CBD. State policy changes were made to allow for alternative placement methods (a new diagnostic tool and high school transcripts) and to update the state's Comprehensive Articulation Agreement (to create a highly structured program of study for transfer students).

Alison Kadlec and Isaac Rowlett of Public Agenda add a unique perspective to this volume. After leading engagement processes—and facilitating conversations with faculty, staff, and administrators—at colleges across the country, they bring their lens to the many factors that can support a reform process and those that can halt one. They cite factors such as size, access to resources, geographic position, policy environment, governance structure, multiple missions, the large proportion of adjunct faculty without the privileges of stable employment, and institutional culture and climate. A clear message that emerges is that change is not technical work; the human dimension of reform is quite powerful and needs great attention.

Katherine L. Hughes
Andrea Venezia
Editors

Reference

Phillips, B. C., & Horowitz, J. E. (Eds.). (2013). *New Directions for Community Colleges: No. 164. The college completion agenda: Practical approaches for reaching the big goal.* San Francisco, CA: Jossey-Bass.

KATHERINE L. HUGHES *is the executive director of Community College and Higher Education Initiatives at the College Board.*

ANDREA VENEZIA *is an associate professor of public policy and administration and the executive director of the Institute for Higher Education Leadership & Policy at California State University, Sacramento.*

1

This chapter describes a promising new approach to teaching developmental arithmetic and prealgebra, and presents research findings that demonstrate how a faculty support network helped instructors adopt new teaching strategies and gain confidence in teaching the reformed course.

Redesigning Arithmetic for Student Success: Supporting Faculty to Teach in New Ways

Susan Bickerstaff, Barbara Lontz, Maria Scott Cormier, Di Xu

Among the strategies to improve college completion, reforms to course curricula and pedagogy may be among the most challenging to implement. Faculty bring unique knowledge, skills, and dispositions to their classrooms, and individual instructors differ in their willingness and ability to adopt new instructional approaches. Further, long-held norms in higher education encourage faculty autonomy and independence in ways that stymie collaborative efforts to improve curriculum and pedagogy.

Yet refining classroom practice holds significant promise to improve outcomes for students (Ingvarson, Meiers, & Beavis, 2005). This is particularly true in developmental education, where students may benefit from a learning environment that is expressly tailored to their academic and nonacademic needs (Karp, 2011; Perin, 2013). Thus an increasing number of reforms ask faculty to apply new strategies and take on new roles in the developmental education classroom. For example, in mathematics these include Carnegie's Statway, the Dana Center's New Mathways Project, the CUNY Start program, and Path2Stats. To secure buy-in, increase instructor comfort with these approaches, and facilitate high-quality implementation, faculty development structures and practices are needed to support faculty to make changes to their teaching practice.

This chapter presents a case study of a redesign of a developmental arithmetic and prealgebra course titled *Concepts of Numbers for Arithmetic and Prealgebra* at Montgomery County Community College (MCCC) in Blue Bell, Pennsylvania. The course seeks to foster students' conceptual

New Directions for Community Colleges, no. 167, Fall 2014 © 2014 Wiley Periodicals, Inc.
Published online in Wiley Online Library (wileyonlinelibrary.com) • DOI: 10.1002/cc.20106

understanding of numbers through an instructional approach that differs significantly from what is commonly seen in traditional postsecondary mathematics classes. Findings for this chapter draw on data from a mixed-method research project studying the implementation and outcomes of the course. We begin with a detailed description of the course curriculum and pedagogy and the story of its implementation at MCCC. We then present qualitative analysis, demonstrating that while instructors faced challenges in adopting new pedagogies, a faculty support network helped them try new strategies and gain confidence with the reform. The chapter concludes with a summary of quantitative analyses, which show that *Concepts of Numbers* has improved outcomes for students referred to arithmetic at MCCC. Overall, the lessons learned from the implementation have implications for increasing the success of students referred to developmental math and for supporting faculty to make changes to their pedagogy across a range of disciplines and college contexts.

Research Context: Addressing the Challenges of Students Referred to Developmental Arithmetic

Nationally, approximately 60% of incoming community college students place into developmental mathematics courses, but only about one third ever move on to college-level mathematics (Bailey, Jeong, & Cho, 2010). At MCCC between 2003 and 2008, success rates for the arithmetic/prealgebra course were between 35% and 45%, among the lowest of any course at the college. Based on these outcomes, it was clear to Barbara Lontz, the creator of *Concepts of Numbers*, that developmental arithmetic was a barrier to degree attainment and needed to be addressed.

Lontz began the reform process with an extensive investigation of arithmetic and prealgebra courses, including the review of over 50 textbooks. This search revealed that these courses were all taught by progressing through a sequence of topics, such as whole numbers, fractions, decimals, percents, signed numbers, and solving basic equations. Within this format, algorithms are presented by instructors; students practice these procedures and ultimately demonstrate mastery with skill assessments. However, students who struggle in arithmetic typically have difficulty connecting one topic to another. Students reported to Lontz and her colleagues that they spent hours on long homework sets practicing procedures, but they did not understand how particular topics fit together. For instance, they were unable to understand how fractions relate to decimals and decimals to percents. To them, mathematics was a collection of rules with many different algorithms to memorize and apply in order to obtain the correct answers. Previous attempts at MCCC to improve developmental math courses (through learning communities and supplemental instruction) did not address this lack of connections, nor did they fundamentally alter instructors' teaching style. Therefore, Lontz envisioned a radical change to both curriculum and instructional delivery.

Concepts of Numbers sets out to address the challenges of students referred to arithmetic in two ways. First it presents course content thematically rather than topically. This reordering is designed explicitly to help students make connections across ideas that may have seemed disparate previously. This focus addresses the concern that most math students understand procedures not concepts, and thus cannot build on them (Givvin, Stigler, & Thompson, 2011). For example, fractions, decimals, and percents appear together in almost every chapter of the course text, which reinforces their relationship to one another. Second, it employs a discovery-based pedagogy that explicitly builds on students' prior knowledge, allowing them to organize their thinking around existing schemas and to clarify concepts they did not understand in the past (Benson & Findell, 2002; Epstein, 1998). Combined, these two components aim to increase students' confidence and foster a newfound appreciation of how numbers work.

Research Design

Concepts of Numbers was examined as part of *Scaling Innovation,* an implementation and research project that investigated how instructional reforms in developmental education are initiated, adapted, and scaled. We draw on two categories of data for this mixed-method analysis. The first is student transcript data from 2,169 students attempting arithmetic at MCCC between fall 2008 and fall 2011. The data set includes student demographics, English and math placement test scores, courses taken and grades received, as well as information on each course, such as course number, course section number, subject, and delivery format. During the time period under investigation, MCCC offered arithmetic/prealgebra using both the reformed and traditional curricula. Students were unaware of which type of section they were enrolled in, allowing for a quasi-experimental design comparing outcomes of students enrolled in *Concepts* with those enrolled in sections using the traditional approach. The second category is qualitative data focused on faculty experiences with the reform. Specifically we analyze 11 interviews with MCCC developmental math faculty and a range of institutional, curricular, and professional developmental documents including written faculty reflections. We also draw on information gleaned from classroom observations and observations of faculty development activities at MCCC and two other colleges implementing *Concepts.*

A Closer Look at the *Concepts* Curriculum

A unique feature of *Concepts* is its innovative course textbook, written by Lontz and published by Pearson. It is comprised of eight units covering the material typically taught in an arithmetic/prealgebra course. These units include: History of Math, The Real Number System, Comparisons, Addition, Subtraction, Multiplication, Division, and Combinations. When students place into arithmetic, they often feel demoralized, assuming they will begin with the traditional arithmetic topics and instructional methods they equate with their lack of past success. Yet the new textbook begins differently. The first unit focuses on the history of math, including information on African, Egyptian, Roman, and Babylonian numeration systems. Students see how our present numeration system evolved from the ideas of many cultures and nations. In addition to laying the foundation for the connections that will be made throughout the semester, this unit was created to promote a positive tone in the class. A new beginning to the course promotes a different understanding of the nature of mathematics and aims to create hope in students that they will experience new, better results.

In the second unit, students investigate all real numbers. By locating various types of numbers on the number line and classifying them as whole numbers, integers, rational or irrational, students begin to see relationships between types of numbers. For example, they begin to see that fractions are no different from decimals—rather, they represent different forms of the same quantity, providing a viable alternative to students' previous negative experiences in math and dispelling myths such as "I can't do fractions." In unit three, numbers are compared using "less than," "greater than," or "equal to." This establishes the premise that it is easier to compare like quantities, providing a meaningful purpose for changing numbers to equivalent forms.

These opening units provide a foundation for the four operations: addition, subtraction, multiplication, and division. All of the arithmetic topics covered in a traditional course are included but rearranged within these conceptual units. For instance, students learn how to add fractions, decimals, signed numbers, and algebraic terms as a collective group. In the next unit, the focus is on subtraction. The course ends with a combination unit that deals with multiple-step problems, synthesizing many of the skills introduced and learned in the course.

Once the history of math has been presented, discovery becomes the main teaching tool. Instead of taking the traditional approach to teaching algorithms, in which the instructor presents definitions, provides examples, and then assigns practice problems, *Concepts* asks students to solve problems by drawing on previous mathematical experiences and knowledge before a rule is given. Adult students referred to arithmetic have holes in their mathematical knowledge, but most have been exposed to the course content in their previous educational experiences. There are always some students in the class who know something about each lesson. When the teacher facilitates discussion among students through the discovery approach, that prior knowledge emerges.

Under this model, instructors encourage students to experiment. By looking at patterns, students discover algorithms as shortcuts. Rules are reconceptualized as memory aids and may or may not be used, depending on the student. Formulas are applied only when necessary. A calculator is a tool to be used only when the calculations become cumbersome, which is rare. Instructors listen to student discussion in class as a means to answer the important question—do they understand? If they do not, then the teacher must tailor class discussions to fill in the blanks and bridge any gaps that remain. Students are involved in the learning process: They ask questions, they are given time to ponder, and their wrong answers are nonetheless considered in class discussion. *Concepts* instructors thus allow students to take ownership for what they are discovering and become active participants in their education.

The *Concepts* textbook has a number of features to facilitate this approach to teaching and learning. For example, the text has minimal narrative and explanation, which facilitates the teacher's use of the discovery approach. Having less prescription allows the lesson to evolve according to the needs and knowledge of the students in the class. The number of homework problems is radically reduced as compared to a traditional textbook. Homework problems are intended to help students assess their own understandings rather than to drill procedures. Faculty teaching *Concepts* report an increase in completed assignments and more consistent attendance, compared with students in traditional arithmetic courses. They attribute this change in students' academic behavior partially to the smaller homework sets. For students or instructors who believe that additional practice is needed, supplemental problems are available in a workbook format and via an online resource aligned with the text. The layout of the textbook is intended to support first-time college students. For example, assignments are found on blue pages; white pages are for instruction and class work. This distinction makes clear to students the expectations for what should be completed outside of class.

Reform Implementation: Moving From Pilot to Scale

Over the span of four years, *Concepts* moved from being a single section pilot to the only arithmetic course offered at MCCC. In fall 2008, *Concepts* was first piloted at MCCC in one arithmetic section after the proposed course redesign had been shared with math faculty and vetted by the mathematics department. Course outcomes from this first semester indicated strong pass rates and suggested this might be a promising approach. Subsequently, the course was piloted in a single section through the fall 2009. During this time, the course text was formalized and revised. In spring 2010, the number of *Concepts* sections was expanded to 14 out of 26 sections. Positive course pass rates prompted the department to further expand to 20 sections in fall 2010. By this time, a significant subset of MCCC math faculty had taught *Concepts*, including a cadre of full-time faculty and adjuncts who were each teaching between one and three sections each semester. With this

NEW DIRECTIONS FOR COMMUNITY COLLEGES • DOI: 10.1002/cc

momentum as a backdrop, in fall 2011 the department voted to replace the traditional arithmetic/prealgebra course with *Concepts*.

As *Concepts* expanded at MCCC, the orientation of new faculty was a critical activity for ensuring that faculty implemented the curriculum as designed. The course's reorganization of subject matter and, most importantly, the change in teaching methods required faculty to move away from a lecture, drill, and practice approach. To change from a lecture-based mode of instruction to a discovery-facilitation format requires time, practice, and support from those with some experience.

Beginning in spring 2010, each new *Concepts* instructor was oriented in a one-to-one or small group meeting before the start of the semester. Faculty were encouraged to reach out to one another with questions, and informal conversations among *Concepts* faculty about the curriculum and discovery approach were not uncommon. However, it soon became evident that the "once and done" orientations only touched the surface of the range of issues *Concepts* faculty might face. They also became increasingly unwieldy as new course sections were added each semester. In addition, last minute course assignments and turnover among adjuncts and tutors made it challenging to ensure that all instructors were adequately prepared, particularly within an orientation system facilitated by a single person. Critically, one-to-one orientations neglected the ongoing needs of returning *Concepts* instructors. To address these needs and to assist instructors in their use of the discovery approach, which many reported as challenging, faculty leadership developed a unique and in-depth learning opportunity to support changes to classroom practice.

Connecting *Concepts* Faculty for In-Depth and Innovative Professional Development

During the 2011–2012 academic year, MCCC refined *Concepts*, expanded faculty development, and supported other colleges in its adoption through funds provided by *Scaling Innovation*. Part of this process involved creating a *Concepts* implementation team comprised of three faculty members. In spring 2012, the team launched CON-NECT (Concepts of Numbers— Networking Educators' Collaborative Thoughts) to create more intensive and ongoing support for faculty teaching *Concepts*. During the first semester, seven MCCC instructors—representing a range of experiences (full-time, adjunct, and varying levels of experience with the course)— volunteered to join the group and met five times to discuss topics related to teaching the course. This model was replicated in fall 2012 and spring 2013 with different groups of *Concepts* faculty; over the course of the three semesters, most full-time and adjunct instructors who regularly teach the course as well as representatives from the tutoring center participated in CON-NECT.

NEW DIRECTIONS FOR COMMUNITY COLLEGES • DOI: 10.1002/cc

One of the functions of CON-NECT was to support ongoing course refinement efforts. Each cohort offered feedback on the textbook and other course materials, and their input shaped subsequent revisions. The group contributed to the assessment of learning outcomes. CON-NECT faculty were invited to administer a common multiple choice final exam in their classes, which was used to identify areas of weakness in the curriculum. The data from this assessment guided subsequent discussions of course materials and teaching practices. For a less resource-intensive and more sustainable approach to orienting new *Concepts* faculty at MCCC and other institutions, the implementation team developed a stand-alone orientation PowerPoint presentation with a voice-over. CON-NECT participants' feedback on this resource was instrumental in its development and refinement.

To explore the discovery pedagogy of *Concepts* in depth, CON-NECT participants viewed and discussed classroom video from *Concepts* classes, gave teaching demonstrations on lessons identified to be challenging, reflected regularly in an e-journal that was shared with the group, and observed another faculty member's *Concepts* class. In addition, CON-NECT offered a venue for more general discussion of teaching and learning. Participants discussed their participation at conferences and read articles and books on topics related to teaching developmental mathematics. At the conclusion of the semester, CON-NECT faculty wrote a culminating reflection paper documenting what impact the group had had on them as educators.

At MCCC these types of activities continue although the refinement grant ended and CON-NECT has formally disbanded. Participants from all three cohorts informally continue to have conversations about the discovery approach and conceptual learning via email and in person. Their input was critical to the development of a new edition of the textbook that includes faculty teaching tips, supplemental and review exercises, computer-based support, a glossary of terms, more application problems, better graphics, and more challenging exercises. Now *Concepts* instructors are invited to attend biannual meetings to provide continued input into course improvements and to offer and receive support from colleagues.

Supporting Pedagogical Change: Lessons Learned From *Concepts*

The story of *Concepts* at MCCC suggests that a motivated group of faculty willing to try something new can successfully launch and scale a substantial change to curriculum and pedagogy. Interviews reveal that faculty enjoy teaching the course, and they believe students enjoy learning arithmetic in *Concepts*. Yet faculty also report significant challenges in adapting their teaching styles to this course. These challenges, and the way that CON-NECT supported faculty to experiment and embrace new ways of teaching, are relevant for reformers working to improve instruction in higher education.

NEW DIRECTIONS FOR COMMUNITY COLLEGES • DOI: 10.1002/cc

The primary challenge faculty reported in teaching *Concepts* was their uncertainty about how to implement the discovery approach. For example, one instructor with several semesters of experience teaching the course explained that he was allowing "more conversation" in class, but he was still not sure if this was really facilitating discovery. Instructors reported that it is difficult to allow students to take the lead, particularly when the instructors have refined their explanations of mathematical rules over the course of their careers. As one instructor described, "I have ways of explaining a concept beautifully, but I'm learning they may need to make mistakes in order to understand the material." Another instructor, halfway through his first semester teaching *Concepts*, admitted that he was spending much of the class time lecturing, largely because he was afraid students might fail if the information was not presented to them.

Many interviewees reported that it was only after they had begun participating in CON-NECT that they gained confidence in the discovery approach. As one instructor explained, "When I first went through the [one-on-one] orientation, I wasn't ready to hear it. The first time I remember getting [the discovery approach] was in a CON-NECT meeting." Overall, instructors reported a deeper understanding of the rationale for the redesign, the goal of the course, and teaching methods for building on student knowledge as a result of CON-NECT. Furthermore, faculty described increasing comfort with facilitating class discussions, moving away from lecture, and allowing students to take responsibility for their learning.

The ongoing nature of CON-NECT, as compared to a single orientation session, provided participants with more in-depth information about the instructional approach. In addition to the intensity, two features of CON-NECT seem salient in providing instructors the support they needed to make changes to their practice. First, the group offered participants visible examples of discovery learning through classroom observations, video review, and teaching demonstrations. "Seeing" the curriculum in action appears to be essential for faculty to adopt a new teaching style. Second, CON-NECT allowed for self-reflection on pedagogy in ways not typically afforded in higher education. Faculty leaders were intentional in modeling self-reflection and vulnerability (e.g., in video recording their own classrooms for analysis) and, in doing so, fostered a sense of collegial trust which grew over the course of the semester. This set the tone for nonevaluative, constructive self- and peer-feedback in the e-journals, peer observations, and reflection papers. One instructor reported: "[The] sharing established a sense of connectedness and refreshed my outlook by allowing me to analyze my personal teaching style and see what I am doing right and what I need to enhance." Participants reported that these activities had a profound impact on their teaching practice.

The lessons learned from faculty teaching in *Concepts of Numbers* have implications for other reforms in other courses and other disciplines. The features of CON-NECT correspond to features of high-quality professional

NEW DIRECTIONS FOR COMMUNITY COLLEGES • DOI: 10.1002/cc

learning opportunities identified in previous research (e.g., Garet, Porter, Desimone, Birman, & Yoon, 2001). The work of the group was *meaningful*, as faculty engaged in substantive discussions about the course (including edits to the textbook), and their conversations were highly *contextualized* (as they discussed specific features of practice highlighted in videos and observations). Additionally, participants were provided significant *structure and guidance* in how to reflect on their practice, which is important because many faculty have little experience talking about their pedagogy. In these ways CON-NECT provides a model that could be adapted to support faculty to change or refine their teaching in both reform and nonreform contexts.

Sustaining Change: Improving the Outcomes for Students in Arithmetic and Beyond

Concepts course pass rates indicate that this new curricular and pedagogical approach is effective for many students referred to the lowest level of developmental mathematics. Comparative analysis completed for this study shows that students enrolled in *Concepts* ($N = 866$) were more likely to be successful than their peers enrolled in the traditional arithmetic/prealgebra course ($N = 1,303$). Specifically, we find that *Concepts* students were more likely to earn a C or higher, less likely to withdraw from the course, and more likely to enroll in algebra, the subsequent developmental math course (for a full description of the methods and findings, please see the forthcoming Community College Research Center Working Paper "Concepts of Numbers: Improving Outcomes in Arithmetic Through Curricular and Pedagogical Reform"). These analyses control for student and course-level characteristics, including student scores on the placement exam. The results suggest that many students benefit from a conceptually oriented curriculum and an instructional approach that aims to allow student understandings of mathematics to emerge.

However, analysis of longer term outcomes suggests the need to look beyond individual course-level reforms to find ways to improve learning and classroom experiences at every stage of a student's college career. In our sample, students enrolled in *Concepts* and their peers in the traditional model completed algebra and gatekeeper math courses at approximately the same rate. During the follow-up period, they did not differ in the total number of college-level credits earned. Many college instructors from across disciplines are experimenting with new ways of teaching to meet their students' needs; however, most often this occurs in isolation, resulting in improvements for individual classrooms rather than in a coordinated increase in success across the college (Nakabugo & Sieborger, 2001). Infrastructure like CON-NECT, which promotes in-depth and ongoing collaborative opportunities for self-reflection on pedagogy, has the potential to impact larger numbers of faculty and thus larger numbers of students, potentially improving student learning and outcomes across course sequences in developmental education and beyond.

References

Bailey, T., Jeong, D. W., & Cho, S. W. (2010). Referral, enrollment and completion in developmental education sequences in community colleges. *Economics of Education Review, 29*(2), 255–270.

Benson, S., & Findell, B. (2002). A modified discovery approach to teaching and learning abstract algebra. In E. Maycock & A. Hibbard (Eds.), *Innovations in teaching abstract algebra* (pp. 11–18). Washington, DC: Mathematical Association of America.

Epstein, J. (1998). Cognitive development in an integrated mathematics and science program. *Journal of College Science Teaching, 27*(3), 194–201.

Garet, M. S., Porter, A. C., Desimone, L., Birman, B. F., & Yoon, K. S. (2001). What makes professional development effective? Results from a national sample of teachers. *American Educational Research Journal, 38*(4), 915–945.

Givvin, K., Stigler, J., & Thompson, B. (2011). What community college developmental mathematics students understand about mathematics, Part II: The interviews. *MathAMATYC Educator, 2*(3), 4–18.

Ingvarson, L., Meiers, M., & Beavis, A. (2005). Factors affecting the impact of professional development programs on teachers' knowledge, practice, student outcomes & efficacy. *Education Policy Analysis Archives, 13*(10), 1–28.

Karp, M. M. (2011). *Toward a new understanding of non-academic student support: Four mechanisms encouraging positive student outcomes in the community college* (CCRC Working Paper No. 28). New York, NY: Columbia University, Teachers College, Community College Research Center.

Nakabugo, M. G., & Sieborger, R. (2001). Curriculum reform and teaching in South Africa: Making a paradigm shift. *International Journal of Educational Development, 21*, 53–60.

Perin, D. (2013). Best practices in teaching writing for college and career readiness. In S. Graham, C. A. MacArthur, & J. Fitzgerald (Eds.), *Best practices in writing instruction* (pp. 48–72). New York, NY: The Guilford Press.

SUSAN BICKERSTAFF *is a postdoctoral research associate at the Community College Research Center at Teachers College, Columbia University.*

BARBARA LONTZ *is an assistant professor of mathematics at Montgomery County Community College, PA.*

MARIA SCOTT CORMIER *is a postdoctoral research associate at the Community College Research Center at Teachers College, Columbia University.*

DI XU *is a postdoctoral research associate at the Community College Research Center at Teachers College, Columbia University.*

2

This chapter tells a story of course reform, describing in a fresh and candid way the steps taken toward change and the results achieved. The authors emphasize that instructors need considerable support in order to teach differently, as well as underscore the need to consider scalability of reform even at the pilot stage.

Steps and Missteps: Redesigning, Piloting, and Scaling a Developmental Writing Program

Peter Adams, Donna McKusick

By most obvious standards, the Accelerated Learning Program (ALP) at the Community College of Baltimore County (CCBC) has been a great success. We first offered a few pilot sections of ALP in fall of 2007 and the results surprised us: more than 70% of the students in ALP passed the developmental course *and* the credit composition course as compared to around 33% of students in the traditional developmental English courses. A few years later, these results were confirmed by a rigorous study conducted by the Community College Research Center (CCRC; Jenkins, Speroni, Belfield, Jaggars, & Edgecombe, 2010). Thus, we went to work doubling the number of sections we offered each year and assisting colleges across the country that wanted to give ALP a try. Today we offer more than 200 sections each year at CCBC, and 152 colleges across the country have begun offering sections as well.

Yes, ALP has, in many ways, been a great success, but in this chapter we wish to tell the whole story, warts and all. Improving developmental education is critical for our students and for higher education's crucial role in promoting an egalitarian society, a society in which all citizens have a chance, if they are willing to work hard, to improve their life situations. The importance of this work compels us to include in this chapter both the steps we took in achieving a major improvement in developmental writing and the missteps we made along the way so that others embarking on this work can learn from our mistakes.

Data Made Us Do It

In a strange way, the story of ALP begins with the purchase of an Apple IIe computer. In 1987, the college bought this computer for the writing

New Directions for Community Colleges, no. 167, Fall 2014 © 2014 Wiley Periodicals, Inc.
Published online in Wiley Online Library (wileyonlinelibrary.com) • DOI: 10.1002/cc.20107

program. Knowing we didn't want to use it for grammar drills, we thrashed around to find another use for it. Taking an idea from a colleague in the Business Division, we thought we might create a database of students who took writing courses to explore a phenomenon we had observed and often discussed. We (Peter, who was then coordinator of the writing program, and Donna, who was coordinator of developmental education) could not understand why we had so many more sections of developmental English than we did of freshman composition. What happened to all of those developmental students? We knew from experience (by simply peeking into classrooms at about the 10th week) that we were losing quite a few students to in-semester attrition, but why? Along with the help of a work-study student, the coordinator of the writing program entered student names and IDs, placement scores, and grades received in each writing course into the computer, resulting in a mini-transcript of just writing assessment and English grades for each student.

About four years later, we were horrified at what we learned: only about one student out of three who started in our upper-level developmental writing course ever passed first-year composition. We knew we had to do better than this. The low success rates we had discovered led us to question whether the basic structure of developmental education was flawed. We wondered whether this structure—placing developmental students in courses for which they usually received no college credit, in which there were no role models who were stronger writers, and which often involved their being prevented from taking most credit courses—was the main cause of the low success rates. We thought that perhaps we would get better results if we devised a model that allowed developmental writers to enroll directly in first-year composition, with some kind of support.

At this point, what we've taken to calling the "lost decade" ensued. In about a 10-year span of time, three separate colleges in Baltimore County were merged into one very large college, and a series of presidents came and went. When we emerged from this period of turmoil, a new leadership team arrived with a public commitment to developmental education. An English Department committee was encouraged to propose a new approach that would result in more developmental students enrolling in and completing freshman composition. Our goal had changed from completion of developmental to enrollment in and completion of the "gateway" credit course, English 101. So we began looking for better models.

Settling on a Model

At Arizona State University in the early 1990s, John Ramage, Dave Schwalm, and later Greg Glau (2007) had initiated the Stretch Program, under which developmental writers were placed in special sections of first-year composition that met for three hours a week for two semesters. Students in the Stretch Program not only improved their success rate in first-year composition but also in the second semester composition course. Meanwhile, at the University of South Carolina, Rhonda Grego and Nancy Thompson (1996) had developed a model they called "studio" in which developmental students were allowed to enroll in first-year composition and also to attend a "studio" section of just 10 students who met once a week to discuss writing projects they were working on. A little earlier, at Evergreen State College in Washington, the learning communities model was developed, a model under which a cohort of students took two or more courses together. The effect of these communities on engagement and retention was promising (Smith, 2001).

Looking for a way to improve our low success rates at CCBC, we combined what seemed to us to be the strongest features of stretch, studio, and learning communities with a few ideas of our own and proposed the new model we call the Accelerated Learning Program.

Based on the data from 1993, a committee composed of the English Department head, the dean of developmental education, and the two coordinators of developmental writing decided it was time to propose a model for developmental writing at CCBC that involved mainstreaming developmental writers into first-year composition in some way. A committee of volunteers was appointed to write a proposal for the department. After considering five different models during spring of 2007, the committee recommended the model we ended up calling ALP.

Under this model, a developmental student would be placed in a designated section of first-year composition, where she would be joined by seven other developmental students. Those eight developmental students would be joined by 12 students whose placement was first-year composition. The eight developmental students would also enroll in a developmental course that would meet for three hours a week with the same instructor. In other words, those eight students would meet together for six hours a week with the same instructor, half that time with just their group of eight.

Why ALP?

Using the data to guide us, our goal was to create a model that would result in more students attempting and completing the "gateway course" of English 101. We identified five factors, many of which we later discovered fit into the productive persistence model developed by the Carnegie Foundation for the Advancement of Teaching and Learning (Carnegie Foundation, n.d.):

1. Because they would actually be enrolled in the college-level writing course, students would feel greater engagement with the college and would feel less doubt about whether they belonged in college. We know from the work of the Carnegie Foundation that a student's

sense of belonging is a fundamental factor in productive persistence (Carnegie Foundation, n.d.).

2. Because students would be in the first-year composition class with other students who are first-year composition level, they will have access to role models who are stronger writers and more savvy about "doing college."

3. Because students would be taking their developmental writing class concurrently with first-year composition, they would no longer see it as an obstacle keeping them from their goal; instead they would see it as a course that is genuinely helpful to them as they take first-year composition and relevant to their success. In other words, the developmental course is contextualized to the credit course, making it immediately relevant and further motivating the students (McKusick, 2012).

4. Taking two courses as a cohort, the eight developmental students would develop a community and feel more engagement, more connection not only to one another but also to the college (Tinto, 1997).

5. Because of the small class size in the developmental class, the instructor would be able to work on the individual needs of the students, both academic and noncognitive. They would more easily be able to create "information networks" that would enhance their persistence (Karp, Hughes, & O'Gara, 2010), and they would gain valuable noncognitive skills for success. Again, addressing these noncognitive needs fits into the productive persistence model (Carnegie Foundation, n.d.) and other models of success that suggest that the student has to have the skills to "do" college to be successful (Bickerstaff, Barragan, & Rucks-Ahidiana, 2012).

First Steps, First Missteps

While the English Department readily agreed to our proposal for a pilot of ALP, the vice president for instruction had one major reservation: the college could not afford to run sections with just eight students. Of course, the VP would let us run a few sections, but what would be the point if the model wasn't "scalable," if the college could not afford to offer it even if it worked. Just as it appeared that the entire project was going to be scrapped, Peter came up with a compromise that may have been a mistake. He suggested that, even though the developmental class would meet three hours a week and even though the students would pay for a three-credit course, the faculty members would receive only two credits toward their teaching load. The VP agreed to this proposal quickly, but now the faculty would have to be convinced. Peter thought the small class size and the fact that the class was not really a separate "preparation" made the two credits of compensation reasonable, and in the early years when the faculty teaching ALP were highly motivated, the compromise worked.

Sensing that there were some faculty who didn't mind if we conducted a pilot as long as they could continue to teach the traditional course the way they always had, and hearing that some faculty were arguing that they thought student "choice" was important, when we proposed the ALP model to the English Department we agreed that students should have a choice and that we would never scale up to 100% ALP; we would always offer some sections of the traditional stand-alone version of developmental writing. Seven years later, this concession would come back to bite us.

Early Successes, Early Warts

During the first semester, an ad hoc advisory group was formed to support the faculty teaching in the program. Meeting in informal locations, the group would discuss the teaching trials and triumphs. One faculty member shared that ALP was the best teaching experience she had ever had, that it was the kind of experience that she had come into the teaching profession for in the first place. Challenges related to teaching mechanics were shared, and faculty learned how to better integrate grammar instruction into actual papers rather than teach it in an isolated fashion. At other times, the discussion turned to generation of paper topics and integrating reading with writing. Finally, the small class size allowed the group to explore the difficult life issues common to developmental students. A group of "advisors" from other areas of the college, areas such as financial aid, or counseling, or the business or allied health faculties, volunteered to visit classes when needed and provide consultation.

At the end of our first tenuous semester, we were elated at our results. About two thirds of the students passed the freshman composition course that they concurrently enrolled in with the developmental course, more than double the percentage for students taking these courses in the traditional manner.

Forging ahead with these early successes, we doubled the number of sections offered. With increased numbers, we began to also see challenges. Increasingly, getting the right balance of eight ALP students and 12 101-level students in the English 101 sections was problematic. Our registrar came up with the solution: We would have our course management system treat the eight ALP seats as one section of English 101 with a class size of eight and a prerequisite of placement in the upper-level developmental writing course. The system would identify the 12 seats for 101-level students as a different section with a class size of 12 and a prerequisite of placement in English 101. Then we would have the two sections meet in the same classroom, at the same time, with the same instructor. Suddenly our registration difficulties melted away to a handful each semester.

We also began to face some policy questions. An early, difficult decision had been whether to permit all developmental writing students whose placement test results fell within the course range to enroll, or only the top half. Again, data ultimately answered the question. It did not significantly matter where a student scored on the Accuplacer in terms of ALP success.

Finally, and most importantly, after scaling up according to plan in the early years by doubling the number of sections every year, we began to hit a snag. Faculty members were increasingly unhappy with the compensation rate of two credits for three credit hours of work. This was especially an issue for adjunct faculty, who work very hard for very low wages and for whom working three hours for two hours of pay was not very appealing. Finally, in spring of 2013, as we realized that ALP was working so well, we were willing to try it with slightly larger class sizes. We proposed to the administration that we raise the class size to 10 and the compensation to three credits. While the effect of this change on the success of the program has been minimal, our ability to recruit ALP faculty improved dramatically.

As we began to scale up ALP, we observed success that exceeded our initial hopes (Adams, Gearhart, Miller, & Roberts, 2009). Needing to validate these successes beyond our own descriptive statistics, we turned to the Community College Research Center (CCRC), which generously agreed to study our program. The results of the CCRC study (Cho, Kopko, Jenkins, & Jaggars, 2012) were again very promising and confirmed our instinct that we would be preparing many faculty, both at CCBC and at other colleges, to teach ALP, once the word got out.

Teaching to Learn, Learning to Teach

From the beginning, we had offered a two-to-three-hour orientation for new ALP faculty each summer and each January. In fall of 2011, as we reached 80 sections of ALP, we were using a large number of new faculty, most of whom were adjuncts. As our summer orientation came to an end, the new faculty began to complain: they didn't feel they were adequately prepared to teach this new course, and we recognized that they were right.

Faculty development is not easy to organize when faculty are spread over three different campuses and are teaching fifteen-credit loads. Our first attempt was to organize an online discussion group called ALPIN. For the fall of 2011, ALPIN was a great success. Three faculty posted examples of activities, assignments, and other classroom materials on the website each week, and a lively online conversation ensued. In the spring semester, participation was a little less robust and tapered off significantly in April and May. By fall of 2012, it was clear that once the novelty of online conversation wore off, ALPIN was not going to work for faculty development at CCBC.

In the early years, the small group of five, or later 10, faculty met often to exchange experiences and ideas. We were figuring out how to most effectively teach the course while we were teaching it—mainly through trial and error. By 2011, while we were far from having a firm, dogmatic pedagogy for ALP, we did have a lot of ideas about what worked and what didn't in the ALP environment. We also had the good fortune to have been awarded a small grant through the William and Flora Hewlett Foundation. Using the funding support from Hewlett and what we had learned from three years of teaching as well as a lot of reading and attending conferences, we developed plans for a five-day, twenty-five-hour faculty institute, which we offered for the first time in August of 2012.

We started our planning for this institute with the question, "How is teaching in an ALP environment different from teaching in a more traditional context?" By the time we had settled on an agenda for the institute, it was clear that we were answering a much broader question—something more like, "What are the best ideas we can come up with for helping students become more successful writers and readers?" Here are the topics we included in the institute:

- overview of ALP;
- backward curriculum design (we ask developmental students to do the same kinds of reading and writing tasks as they are doing in the credit course, only more slowly with more support);
- active learning (we don't rely so heavily on traditional lecture classes, but more often ask students, working in groups, to work on a task that leads them to learn through the activity);
- thinking skills (we emphasize how much effective writing is the result of serious thinking);
- assigning and responding to writing;
- noncognitive issues (ALP faculty recognize that the primary cause of student failure is issues involving their lives and their psychological state and that faculty can help reduce the negative effects of these factors);
- effective editing skills;
- coordinating syllabi from the two courses.

With the institute, we seem to have stumbled onto the right formula for faculty development at CCBC. The institute is scheduled for a week when there are no classes. Faculty members are compensated modestly for attending. Lots of active learning provides an opportunity for faculty to develop materials for their classes the next semester. And, the week is treated as a smorgasbord from which the faculty select just the ideas that appeal to them. There is no requirement for everyone to teach the class in exactly the same way.

The response to the institute was so positive that we scheduled a second one in the fall, another in January, and a fourth in August 2013. Faculty who attended have repeatedly told us that the institute had not only been extremely helpful for teaching ALP but it had also changed the way they would teach all their writing courses.

Scaling Up Is Hard to Do

From the beginning, we built scaling up into our model for ALP. Each year, for the first five years we doubled the number of sections we offered, until, in fall of 2012, we were offering 80 sections of ALP. This growth did not come without difficulties. In 2008–2010, the college was experiencing tremendous enrollment growth. As a result, classroom space was in short supply. To schedule a class of just eight students in a room that can hold 25 was not a good use of resources, so we launched a major effort to locate underused conference rooms and convert them into ALP classrooms, to construct small classrooms in dead space in lobby areas, and to divide some classrooms in half.

We also began to realize that scaling up meant more than simply offering more sections of ALP. It also meant that we had to reduce the number of sections of the traditional developmental writing course, which resulted in fewer classes for those students who did not want ALP and more pressure on the department chair by advisors to leave traditional sections in the schedule. This realization has led to an honest discussion, college-wide, of whether we want ALP to be the only choice for remediation at a given level, a discussion that continues as we move beyond enrolling 60% (1,000 students annually) of the eligible students each year into ALP.

No one, after six years of ALP, is arguing that it is a mistake or that we should stop offering it. However, now that something approaching 60% of eligible students are enrolling in ALP, the momentum for scaling up further is slowing considerably. It's not easy to explain why this is the case.

Some of it involves implementing change in a highly complex institutional setting. For example, we would like to change the messaging that students receive about their options. Instead of telling them, as we do now, that they are placed into English 052 (the traditional course) and that ALP is another option, we could tell them they are placed into ALP, with the traditional course an option for those who can't enroll in six credit hours of English. The "message" flows through many hands on a typical college campus—from the academic departments to the testing center, to the advisors, and eventually to the students. Because it involves many technological systems, from the automated messaging connected with the computer adaptive placement test we administer to the description and entry of placement into the Student Information System, to the automated record keeping that is part of the degree auditing system, such a change in a complex institution like ours can easily take over a year to implement. ALP advocates—focused on the fact that 74% of ALP students are passing English 101 while only 33% of students who take the traditional course have a similar success—are convinced that we should no longer even offer the traditional course. If there are physical or policy difficulties standing in the way of making that happen, we want to find solutions to those difficulties.

NEW DIRECTIONS FOR COMMUNITY COLLEGES • DOI: 10.1002/cc

But other parts of the campus—less focused on ALP's successes—see the difficulties as reasons to slow the growth. Among the difficulties that have been raised at meetings are these:

- Students should have a choice of courses.
- Some students are afraid of English and don't want to take two courses at once or don't want to be "accelerated."
- Some students' schedules make it difficult for them to take ALP.
- Some faculty do not want to teach ALP.
- ALP uses up valuable classroom space.
- We will have difficulty finding enough faculty members to teach all the sections.

What is clear to us is that scaling up involves more than the number of sections offered. As Coburn (2003) has suggested, a consideration of depth as indicated by faculty beliefs and expectations of students, sustainability that outlasts faculty and resource turnover, spread of the underlying philosophy and pedagogy, and ownership by all in the department is critical to the success of the scaling effort.

Lessons Learned

As we reflect on the past seven years of ALP, a number of distinct lessons have emerged. First, implementing ALP requires a champion who is willing to envision a future with improved outcomes for developmental writing students, inspire faculty to make a change, and tackle logistical challenges. This may involve convincing deans or other administrators that the model is worthy of a pilot; encouraging faculty who teach only freshman composition that with training, they too can enjoy working with developmental students; identifying adequate classroom space; working with the advisors so they can better understand and convey the model to students; or working with registration staff to direct students into the right sections.

The second lesson is to take the risk of using the most compelling story of all, the story that the numbers tell, to convince faculty and administrators that change is needed. Data can also tell an encouraging, early narrative of success which can help a fledgling program gain momentum. Gathering these data on an ongoing schedule requires a strong working relationship with the institutional research department.

A third lesson is that early advocates need to form a coalition of supporters from all areas of the college to carry the work forward as part of the complete pathway that every developmental writing student travels. Because this program addresses the whole learner, the coalition of supporters and stakeholders should include faculty from within the department and from other developmental areas, as well as administrators and staff from areas such as advising, counseling, financial aid, registration, scheduling, marketing, and institutional research.

Although many variations of ALP exist in the 152 colleges that have adopted it, most adhere to some fundamental tenets. These include a belief in mainstreaming, because it offers the academic challenge that helps students grow cognitively and reduces opportunities for students to drop out, along with a recognition that the model must provide, through its delivery system, more support in the noncognitive domain. As we have worked with other colleges, we have offered them the lesson that although they will have to carefully shape the model to address internal factors such as faculty workload and departmental organizational structure, they may only get dramatic results if they honor the basic underlying tenets of ALP.

A final lesson we learned was that to be successful, the model has to be scalable both in concept and in reality. To be scalable, it must address many factors from the outset. These include instrumental factors such as faculty workload, physical resources such as classrooms, ease of registration, coherence with policy, and deeper actors achieved through comprehensive, ongoing faculty development that make true believers of the entire college community.

Conclusion

And what about those missteps? In retrospect, it seems that, in order to get approval to pilot ALP, we agreed to some compromises that we probably shouldn't have. It was probably a mistake to agree to ask faculty to teach three hours a week for two hours of compensation. It was also probably a mistake to agree with skeptics that we would never scale ALP up to include all students.

But it is also important to recognize that in those early days we had no idea how successful it would turn out to be. A willingness to make compromises made sense when we badly wanted to try something new, without knowing how successful it would be. Missteps, yes, but understandable when we had no data or experiences to point to. We now know that ALP can change the academic paths of many community college students, and we are eager to share the good news, warts and all.

References

Adams, P., Gearhart, G., Miller, R., & Roberts, A. (2009). The accelerated learning program: Throwing open the gates. *Journal of Basic Writing*, 28(2), 50–69.

Bickerstaff, S., Barragan, M., & Rucks-Ahidiana, Z. (2012). *"I came in unsure of everything": Community college students' shifts in confidence* (CCRC Working Paper No. 48). New York, NY: Columbia University, Teachers College, Community College Research Center.

Carnegie Foundation. (n.d.). Productive persistence. Retrieved from http://www .carnegiefoundation.org/productive-persistence

New Directions for Community Colleges • DOI: 10.1002/cc

Cho, S., Kopko, E., Jenkins, D., & Jaggars, S. S. (2012, December). *New evidence of success for community college remedial English students: Tracking the outcomes of students in the Accelerated Learning Program (ALP)*. Retrieved from http://ccrc.tc.columbia.edu/media/k2/attachments/ccbc-alp-student-outcomes-follow-up.pdf

Coburn, C. (2003). Rethinking scale: Moving beyond numbers to deep and lasting change. *Educational Researcher, 32*(6), 3–12.

Glau, G. (2007). Stretch at 10: A progress report on Arizona State University's stretch program. *Journal of Basic Writing, 26*(2), 30–48.

Grego, R., & Thompson, N. (1996). Repositioning remediation: Renegotiating composition's work in the academy. *College Composition and Communication, 47*, 62–84.

Jenkins, D., Speroni, C., Belfield, C., Jaggars, S. S., & Edgecombe, N. (2010, September). *A model for accelerating academic success of community college remedial English students: Is the Accelerated Learning Program (ALP) effective and affordable?* Retrieved from http://ccrc.tc.columbia.edu/media/k2/attachments/remedial-english-alp-effective-affordable.pdf

Karp, M., Hughes, K., & O'Gara, L. (2010). An exploration of Tinto's integration framework for community college students. *Journal of College Student Retention: Research, Theory, and Practice, 12*(1), 69–86.

McKusick, D. (2012). *Making it real: Using contextualization for student success* (The Cross Papers No. 15). Chandler, AZ: League for Innovation in Community College.

Smith, B. (2001). The challenge of learning communities as a growing national movement. *Peer Review*. Retrieved from http://www.aacu.org/peerreview/pr-fa01/pr-fa01feature1.cfm

Tinto, V. (1997). Classrooms as communities: Exploring the educational character of student persistence. *Journal of Higher Education, 68*(6), 599–623.

PETER ADAMS *is the immediate past director of the Accelerated Learning Program at the Community College of Baltimore County. Currently he provides presentations and consultation to colleges and higher education systems across the country on developmental education.*

DONNA MCKUSICK *is the dean for Developmental Education and Special Academic Programs at the Community College of Baltimore County.*

3

This chapter describes how the authors are using data and professional learning to mobilize change in developmental English and mathematics curricula and pedagogy across multiple community colleges in California.

The California Acceleration Project: Reforming Developmental Education to Increase Student Completion of College-Level Math and English

Katie Hern, with Myra Snell

Nationwide, most community college students are placed into remediation and required to take one or more semesters of non-credit-bearing coursework in reading, writing, and/or mathematics. And though these courses are intended to prepare students for success at the college level, large research studies have shown that the majority of students placed into remediation do not go on to complete college-level requirements in English and math. Indeed, the lower down students start, the lower their completion rates (Bailey, Jeong, & Cho, 2008). In California, just 19% of community college students who begin three or more levels below college-level coursework in writing go on to complete a college-level English course in three years. The figure is a dismal 6% for students who begin three or more levels below college math (California Community Colleges Chancellor's Office, 2012a). Students of color are particularly impacted in the current system, because they are disproportionately placed into the lowest levels of remediation. In math, for example, more than half of all Black and Latino community college students in California are placed three or more levels below college (Perry, Bahr, Rosin, & Woodward, 2010).

As leaders of the California Acceleration Project (CAP), we are working to address this problem by supporting community colleges to redesign their remedial curricula. In partnership with the statewide community college professional development organization 3CSN, funded through grants from the state Chancellor's Office, the Walter S. Johnson Foundation, and LearningWorks, we offer workshops demonstrating that to increase student

NEW DIRECTIONS FOR COMMUNITY COLLEGES, no. 167, Fall 2014 © 2014 Wiley Periodicals, Inc.
Published online in Wiley Online Library (wileyonlinelibrary.com) • DOI: 10.1002/cc.20108

completion of college-level English and math, community colleges must re-think the use of multilevel remedial course sequences, as well as the standardized placement tests used to sort students into these sequences. We share results from established accelerated models of remediation, including single-semester courses open to students with any placement score (Hern, 2012) and models that enable underprepared students to enroll directly into the college-level course with additional, corequisite support (Jenkins, Speroni, Belfield, Jaggars, & Edgecombe, 2010). And because changes to the structure of remediation must be supported by changes in the classroom, we offer a set of instructional design principles to help teachers move away from traditional, decelerated approaches and offer high-challenge, high-support accelerated courses (Hern, 2013).

The project began in June 2010, when we published an article in the newsletter of the California community college system's Research and Planning Group (RP Group), focusing on the problem of attrition in long remedial sequences and the improved results our own colleges were seeing in shortened, redesigned English and math curricula (Hern, 2010). We hoped to spark a statewide conversation and, perhaps, inspire colleges to offer their own accelerated models of English and math. But we recognized that curricular change is difficult, particularly in California, where all 112 community colleges are locally governed. Our first grant proposal included modest goals: by fall 2013, we aimed to give workshops to 40 community colleges and support 5 colleges to pilot accelerated remediation.

We have far exceeded those early goals. As of December 2013, faculty and administrators from almost all of the state's 112 community colleges have participated in CAP workshops, and 42 colleges have offered redesigned accelerated courses in English and math through a yearlong professional development program offered with 3CSN. Even more exciting are the results from early pilots. A third-party evaluation by the RP Group examined 16 colleges that began offering accelerated courses with CAP in 2011–2012 and found that students' odds of completing college-level gateway courses were 2.3 times higher in effective accelerated English pathways than in traditional remediation and 4.5 times higher in accelerated math pathways (Hayward & Willett, 2014). Beyond student outcomes, a fiscal analysis conducted by the National Center for Inquiry and Improvement showed that the accelerated math pathways being piloted in CAP significantly lower colleges' costs-per-completer, enable colleges to reallocate resources from remediation to transferable courses, and offer significant economic benefits to students through reduced book/tuition expenses and wage increases from expedited completion.

This chapter describes key factors that have helped to build the momentum for change across California's community colleges, as well as the challenges we've encountered. We hope that examining a grassroots, faculty-driven reform effort will be useful to community college practitioners both within and beyond California. States with decentralized

NEW DIRECTIONS FOR COMMUNITY COLLEGES • DOI: 10.1002/cc

governance structures might consider whether a similar effort could be built locally. More centralized states might take the lessons we are learning college-by-college and do what California hasn't yet been able to— transform remediation system-wide, so that more effective accelerated pathways are available to all students, not just those lucky enough to get into a pilot section.

Clarity About a Shared Problem

The Community College Research Center study cited previously (Bailey et al., 2008) went a long way toward focusing attention on the tremendous attrition in developmental education nationwide, demonstrating that the lower down students begin, the less likely they are to pass a college-level gatekeeper course. A California-wide study revealed the same basic trends (Perry et al., 2010). But in presentations to faculty, we have found that this research doesn't automatically mobilize people to action. One response we encountered early on was: *We don't have this problem at my college.*

To teachers, attrition in a multicourse sequence has been an invisible problem. We only see the students in our individual classrooms. Some pass, some don't, and when the semester is over, we get a new batch of students. Aside from the few who keep in touch, we don't usually know what happens to students after the semester, and we certainly don't know what happens to students across all sections of our program. For the most part, if we have looked at quantitative data on student outcomes—say, for a program review or federal grant—we have typically focused on pass rates in individual courses, rather than longitudinal cohort studies.

To make the invisible visible, CAP and 3CSN partnered with the RP Group and the California Community Colleges' Chancellor's Office to build a new tool for the statewide data repository: the Basic Skills Cohort Tracker. With a simple online interface, faculty from across the state's 112 community colleges can pull up data on student progression through their basic skills sequences in reading, writing, math, and English as a Second Language (ESL), following cohorts of students from their first enrollment in a given discipline through their completion of transferable college-level courses.

For example, if a faculty member at San Diego's Cuyamaca College wants to know how basic skills math students are doing, and she's especially interested in the ones who start low in the sequence, she can go to the Tracker, format her request with a simple pull-down menu, click View Report, and immediately have her answer: 106 students started three levels below college math in fall 2008, and three years later, three of those students had completed a transferable math course (3%), including repeated attempts (California Community Colleges Chancellor's Office, 2012a). What if she extended the timeframe to five years? Back to the pull-down menu;

NEW DIRECTIONS FOR COMMUNITY COLLEGES • DOI: 10.1002/cc

adjust the end term; view report. Now, it's 7 of those 106 students (7%) (California Community Colleges Chancellor's Office, 2012a).

As we encourage faculty to focus on this problem, we stress that it isn't that their college is doing a bad job, or that they are bad teachers. The Cohort Tracker makes clear that the problem is not only shared by community colleges statewide, but that it is built into the structure of a multilevel course sequence. Basically, the more *opportunities* there are to lose students, the more students community colleges will lose. This is especially true among low-income students, who face multiple pressures pulling them away from school. And it is especially true in remedial math and English courses, where students earn no credit, make no progress toward a longer term credential, and often face material that has frustrated them in the past (grammar, algebra).

Since the debut of the tool in early 2012, we rarely encounter faculty who believe their multilevel remedial sequence is somehow different. And if we do, it's easy to demonstrate that even their college—with its great pedagogy, counseling, tutoring, learning communities, you name it—is losing huge numbers of students inside multiple layers of remediation. We encourage other states—particularly those with decentralized governance structures—to consider developing their own version of the tool. It elegantly demonstrates the need for reform and, going forward, makes it easy for colleges to track the outcomes of redesigned curricula.

Results From Accelerated Models

Early on, as we shared the research showing that the lower down a student is placed, the lower their completion of a gatekeeper course, we'd often hear something like, "Well, what do you expect? They can't even add fractions." In other words, students' placement is an indication of their limited abilities, and these limited abilities are the cause of their low completion rates. Remediation is premised on the idea that students need these courses and that, without them, they cannot handle the challenge of the higher level. Mobilizing faculty for change requires taking on this largely unquestioned belief. Faculty need to see that students do not, in fact, need all those layers of remediation. They need to know that across colleges and instructors, students in redesigned, accelerated remediation have higher completion rates of college-level courses, including students who score low on standardized placement tests.

On the English side, CAP workshops feature results from several established models of acceleration (see the chapter in this volume on the Accelerated Learning Program at the Community College of Baltimore County and Jenkins et al., 2010). At Chabot College in California, developmental students with any placement score can take just a single precollegiate semester of integrated reading and writing instruction. The accelerated class functions as a kind of "junior varsity college English." Students do the same kinds of reading, thinking, and writing required at the higher level, but faculty understand that they are not yet as skilled as more advanced students. The class features longer class periods and more scaffolding than a college-level class, such as activities to help students grapple with challenging readings, in-class writing support, and explicit guidance to acculturate students to the expectations of the college environment.

Descriptive data from the Basic Skills Cohort Tracker show that for more than a decade, students who have chosen Chabot's accelerated single-semester accelerated course have completed college English at rates 23–26 percentage points higher than students who opted for the two-semester remedial pathway (Hern, 2011). A study conducted by CCRC used two kinds of statistical modeling (regression and propensity score matching) to control for preexisting student characteristics and found that, within five years, accelerated students were 17–22 percentage points more likely to complete college English, 7–10 percentage points more likely to have transferred or qualify as "transfer ready," and 4–6 percentage points more likely to have graduated than their nonaccelerated peers (Edgecombe, Jaggars, Xu, & Barragan, 2014).

On the math side, CAP workshops encourage faculty to develop accelerated remediation by first asking *which math* students need for success in their chosen college pathway. Instead of simply repeating all of K–12 mathematics through Algebra II, accelerated math pathways align remediation with the specific college-level math requirements students will take—more extensive algebra for students heading toward calculus, less algebra and more quantitative reasoning and data analysis for students taking statistics or liberal arts math. The pathways approach to math remediation, a centerpiece of recent national recommendations for increasing college completion, is being implemented across the country through the Carnegie Foundation's Statway and Quantway initiatives; the New Texas Mathways Project run by the Charles A. Dana Center at the University of Texas at Austin; and reforms in Colorado, Virginia, North Carolina, Indiana, Florida, and other states (Burdman, 2013; Charles A. Dana Center, Complete College America, Education Commission of the States, Jobs for the Future, 2012).

In California, Los Medanos College was the first to implement an accelerated pathway through statistics, with the launch of Path2Stats in 2009. Path2Stats is a one-semester prestatistics course with no minimum placement score, for students pursuing non-math-intensive majors. Descriptive data from the first several student cohorts showed that completion of college math was three times higher among accelerated students than students in the traditional curriculum. These results are especially impressive given that the Path2Stats group was studied for just one year with no repeats, while the traditional group was studied for three years, including repeated attempts. In other words, Path2Stats tripled the student completion in one third the time (Hern, 2012). Inspired by Los Medanos, most colleges working with

CAP are piloting a local version of an accelerated prestatistics course that replaces two to four courses in the traditional remedial curriculum.

The Need to Rethink Placement

In addition to sharing evidence from successful English and math models, we encourage colleges to be skeptical of the placement tests they're using to sort students into multiple semesters of remediation. Recent research has raised questions about these tests and pointed to the widespread underplacement of students into remediation (e.g., Belfield & Crosta, 2012; Hetts, Fuenmayor, & Rothstein, 2012; Scott-Clayton, 2012). In math, there is the additional problem of curricular misalignment. For students going into non-math-intensive pathways—e.g., humanities and social science majors who take statistics as their quantitative requirement—access to college-level courses is determined by a test of their algebra skills, even though very little algebra is needed for success in these courses. The misalignment inherent in algebra-based testing and remediation suggests a promising direction for the future: redesigning placement processes so that students' algebra skills only determine access to courses where those skills are in fact required.

Among colleges piloting accelerated pathways, faculty often express concern about whether the lowest placed students can handle the demands of an accelerated course one level below college, and some CAP colleges have placed prerequisites on their accelerated courses. Part of the concern is pedagogical—faculty worry about how they can support students who have weak reading or numeracy skills to be successful. This concern is important to address through faculty development (see section to follow), but it can also be examined empirically, by looking at how the lowest placed students perform in accelerated pathways.

In their evaluation of CAP pilot colleges, the RP Group found that students at all levels of remediation, including three and four levels below college, saw gains in accelerated pathways, and the lowest placed students saw the largest relative increases in their completion of college-level gateway courses. "The implication is that students from an array of skill ranges can be prepared for success in transfer-level English or statistics via an effective acceleration implementation," Hayward and Willett (2014, p. 45) conclude. "Further, no specific level was associated with negative outcomes indicating that these accelerated pilots adhered to a 'do no harm' principle" (p. 45).

These findings conflict with many instructors' experience in the classroom, which has convinced them that *some* students need a slower path. They can think of specific individuals, students they *know* would not have made it to college level in one semester. In discussions with these faculty, we don't disagree. We can also recall students who, despite their best efforts, needed more than a semester of developmental work on their reading,

NEW DIRECTIONS FOR COMMUNITY COLLEGES • DOI: 10.1002/cc

writing, and quantitative skills. The problem is that our placement tests do not accurately identify these students.

Outcomes from the Chabot-Las Positas community college district illustrate the weakness of Accuplacer—one of the most widely used placement tests nationally—as a predictor of student capacity. In 2010, we examined eight semesters of data to try to answer a question that often arises among faculty: Should there be a minimum placement score for an accelerated English course? Is there a group of students who are just not successful in the accelerated option? We looked at students who tested below the college English cut score and enrolled in either the single accelerated course or the developmental course two levels below college, examining the relationship between students' Accuplacer scores and their pass rates in either course. We knew that, as a group, accelerated students were more likely to go on to complete college English over time, but we wondered about how students fared in the first developmental course, particularly low-scoring students.

What we found was surprising. Even the lowest scoring students—those scoring below 50 on both the Accuplacer reading and sentence skills tests, comprising less than 5% of the student population in the district—passed the accelerated, one level below English course at a rate of 48%. More surprising, these students *did no better* in the slower paced course two levels below, where their pass rate was 45% (Chabot results presented in Hern, 2011). These are students whose test scores would place them into three or more remedial courses at many institutions, or who might be denied access to college for being "below the floor." And yet, nearly half of them were succeeding in a challenging course one level below college English.

In CAP workshops, we encourage faculty to let go of their certainty that students' placement scores reflect the level of challenge they can—or more importantly, *can't*—handle. And we encourage them to redirect their concerns: Instead of trying to keep weak students out of challenging classes, we argue that they need to be worried about using weak standardized tests to block capable students from courses in which they can be successful, particularly when requiring even a single semester of additional remedial coursework is correlated with significantly lower completion rates.

Policy Challenges to Transforming Math Remediation

Despite these promising results, California community colleges are having difficulty scaling accelerated math pathways because of transfer articulation policies at the University of California and the California State University systems. Current UC and CSU policies prescribe algebra-based remediation for all students, regardless of their intended program of study. In setting their policies, the four-year universities have been inclined to apply a single, high school–based standard of "college readiness" in mathematics, despite the clear mismatch of this standard for transfer students. Having chosen a major and completed 60 transferable college credits—including a rigorous college-level quantitative requirement—community college transfer students have more than demonstrated their readiness for college. Given that they are halfway through college, their high school coursework is no longer an appropriate indicator of their abilities. Nevertheless, current policies serve as a de facto mandate from the four-year universities that community colleges require multiple levels of nontransferable remediation of high school requirements.

While these policies remain in place, the 21 community colleges piloting accelerated statistics pathways with CAP are using an internal mechanism to navigate this obstacle. Partially in response to a lawsuit in the 1990s from the Mexican American Legal Defense Fund, the California community college system has a number of protections in place to ensure that prerequisites don't unfairly and disproportionately block students' access to courses in which they could be successful. One of the protections written into the state's education code is that community colleges must offer prerequisite challenge processes to students who demonstrate "the knowledge or ability to succeed in the course or program despite not meeting the prerequisite" (California Community Colleges Chancellor's Office, 2012b, p. 18). At community colleges piloting statistics pathways, intermediate algebra remains the only official prerequisite for their transferable statistics courses. But when students demonstrate that they have the ability to succeed in statistics through their performance in a new prestats course, colleges are using their prerequisite challenge processes to advance them to the higher level.

The CSU's Chancellor's Office has signaled to community colleges that it considers this process part of our legitimate purview (California Acceleration Project, 2013). But even with these legal mechanisms in place, the current transfer policies are having a chilling effect on the spread of redesigned math pathways (Fain, 2013). Math faculty are a risk-averse group, and they don't tend to like policy gray areas. As we give workshops around the state, the issue of intermediate algebra and transfer articulation is the single most common question to come up from math faculty, and at a number of colleges, interested faculty are waiting to move ahead until the policies change. To scale up these promising innovations, California needs system-level reform to ensure that community colleges have the authority to design effective remedial math pathways, instead of being forced to remediate students in high school work that is irrelevant to the transfer requirements for their major.

Design Principles and Collaborative Faculty Development Networks

One challenge to scaling up accelerated models of English and math is that the new curricula can represent fairly substantial changes to both *what* and *how* faculty have been teaching. A teacher who has been focusing only on grammar exercises and paragraph writing needs support to teach classes in which students read books and write text-based academic essays. If a college is going to integrate formerly separate curricula in reading and writing, the reading teachers need support to help students write, and the writing teachers need support to help students be more successful readers. In redesigned statistics pathways, the changes can be even more profound, because many mathematics faculty have done little to no work in the field of statistics (which some argue is "not even math"). Indeed, some of the faculty who stepped forward to teach the first accelerated prestatistics courses in California had never taught statistics before. Adding complexity to their challenge, there are no textbooks on the market for this kind of class, no time-tested curriculum they can adopt. At times during their first semester, the math faculty in CAP have felt like they were barely a week ahead of their students, the teaching equivalent of being on a high wire without a net.

In supporting faculty to teach accelerated English and math pathways, we do not require them to faithfully adopt a single preset curriculum. Instead, we offer a set of five design principles for teaching in high-challenge, high-support accelerated pathways for underprepared students, principles we have seen be particularly powerful in our own classrooms. Laid out in detail in a recent policy brief from LearningWorks (Hern, 2013), the principles involve engaging students in the same kinds of challenging, higher order tasks they will be asked to do in a college English or statistics course, and providing just-in-time, contextualized remediation on skills needed for the more challenging work (e.g., individualized grammar support as students write essays; pausing to review an algebraic or arithmetic skill needed in a particular data analysis assignment). The principles also stress the need for classroom practices addressing the affective issues that can get in students' way (e.g., fear, fixed mindsets) and the importance of low-stakes, collaborative practice to help students build confidence and mastery before a higher-stakes assessment. These principles help to ground faculty and lower anxiety as they transition to new approaches, without imposing an off-the-shelf curriculum or overly constraining their creativity as teachers.

Another factor that has helped—tremendously—is for faculty to come together in collaborative peer networks to get ideas, energy, and support from one another. With funding from the state and private foundations, the CAP Community of Practice has made the space for this across California. Participating faculty attend three multiday workshops during their first year of teaching a new accelerated class, to learn from teachers who have experience with accelerated models, engage with sample curricular materials, and get specific ideas they can use in their own classrooms. In math, the Community of Practice has been a major venue for addressing the lack of textbooks or established curricula for accelerated prestatistics courses, as participating faculty share materials with one another. The CAP website is also a major resource for faculty transitioning to acceleration, with videos, sample assignments, and magazine-style spotlight articles featuring accelerated classrooms across California (http://cap.3csn.org).

In addition to the larger statewide network, faculty are building local peer-to-peer support networks on their own campuses. At many colleges, the early-initiator faculty who participated in CAP have gone on to support other faculty as colleges increase their accelerated offerings. They lead workshops, write blogs, organize online resource sharing, and keep their office doors open for fellow faculty.

Our work in California has shown that tremendous momentum can be unleashed when teachers are committed to a reform movement. But it also has made clear that when faculty are teaching in a new way, they need support. Policymakers can and should make structural changes to enable more students to complete college-level gateway courses, but to be truly successful, remediation reform must also address what and how faculty are teaching. We urge colleges and state systems to build in intentional resources to support this kind of work.

From Successful Pilots to System-Level Change?

To mobilize for change, faculty need to see that the current remedial system has the unintended consequence of weeding students out of college. They need to understand that students are more capable than our placement tests have led us to believe, and that they can be successful in accelerated models. And they need to believe that if they redesign their curriculum, they won't be setting students up for failure. On the last issue, while data from other colleges help, it is nevertheless a leap of faith to create and teach a new accelerated course, and most teachers go into it with a combination of excitement and fear. They don't want students to fail, and they don't want to fail as teachers. Supportive, peer-led professional development is therefore essential to helping faculty shift from traditional, decelerated models of instruction.

The above factors have made it possible to mobilize faculty from 42 independently governed community colleges to pilot redesigned, accelerated pathways for underprepared students, and early data show these efforts are paying off for students. This is far more than we had hoped for in the early days of the California Acceleration Project, and we are thrilled with the progress that has been made. And yet, it is not enough. Too many students are still disappearing inside long remedial course sequences before making progress on their education goals. The next phase of our work must involve moving beyond pilots to create system-wide change.

In states with more centralized governance, new structures for remediation are being mandated system-wide, sometimes driven by legislation (Florida, Connecticut), at other times by change processes that include faculty (Colorado). But in many of these cases, the perception that reforms are being imposed top-down means that faculty often do not own the change.

NEW DIRECTIONS FOR COMMUNITY COLLEGES • DOI: 10.1002/cc

Structural and policy changes are not supporting changes to instruction and in some cases may be undermined by ground-level implementation.

In California, there has been little to no curricular direction from the top. The legislature and state chancellor's office have provided professional development funding to improve outcomes among underprepared students, but they have imposed no mandates or accountability mechanisms regarding what the reform should look like. Colleges that want to continue requiring students to complete four layers of remediation in reading, writing, and math remain free to do so without interference from the state. The movement to transform remediation is, instead, a grassroots, faculty-led, college-by-college effort. Individual faculty step forward to develop accelerated models for their local context, and they start with a few sections at a time. The faculty leading the effort tend to believe deeply in the changes they're making, and they often report that their love for teaching is reinvigorated as they move away from old models of remediation (Foth, 2013). There's not just "buy-in," there's a deep sense of ownership among participating faculty. And yet, faculty champions often contend with a lack of support from their department and sometimes even active, hostile opposition from other faculty (Bickerstaff & Scaling Innovation Team, 2014; Hayward & Willett, 2014; Hern, 2013). The status quo has inertia on its side, and faculty who oppose curricular change can often block promising reforms or simply refuse to teach in new models.

So how can we shift the balance away from the current, broken system? How do we ensure that effective, accelerated curricula are available to all students, not just those lucky enough to get into a pilot section? Can system leaders, trustees, and administrators incentivize and support colleges to redesign remediation, without undermining faculty ownership and commitment? And can it happen at a pace commensurate with the urgency of the problem? This is a critical question for the next phase of the work to transform remediation on behalf of our students.

References

Bailey, T., Jeong, D. W., & Cho, S. W. (2008, December). *Referral, enrollment, and completion in developmental education sequences in community colleges* (CCRC Working Paper No. 15) (Revised Nov. 2009). New York, NY: Community College Research Center, Teachers College, Columbia University. Retrieved from http://ccrc.tc.columbia.edu/publications/referral-enrollment-completion-developmental-education.html

Belfield, C., & Crosta, P. M. (2012, February). *Predicting success in college: The importance of placement tests and high school transcripts* (CCRC Working Paper No. 42). New York, NY: Community College Research Center, Teachers College, Columbia University. Retrieved from http://ccrc.tc.columbia.edu/publications/predicting-success-placement-tests-transcripts.html

Bickerstaff, S., & Scaling Innovation Team. (2014, February). Faculty orientations toward instructional reform. *Inside-Out: A Publication of the Scaling Innovation Project*. (Issue No. 5). New York, NY: Community College Research Center,

Teachers College, Columbia University. Retrieved from http://www.scalinginnovation
.org/faculty-orientations-toward-instructional-reform/

Burdman, P. (2013). *Changing equations: How community colleges are rethinking college readiness in math.* Oakland, CA: LearningWorks. Retrieved from http://www.learningworksca.org/changingequations/

California Acceleration Project. (2013, April 12). CSU issues statement on intermediate algebra policy and articulation [Blog post]. Retrieved from http://cap.3csn.org/2013/04/12/csu-clarifies-intermediate-algebra-policy/

California Community Colleges Chancellor's Office. (2012a). *Basic Skills Progress Tracker. Management Information Systems Data Mart.* Retrieved from http://datamart.cccco.edu/Outcomes/BasicSkills_Cohort_Tracker.aspx

California Community Colleges Chancellor's Office. (2012b, February 3). *Guidelines for Title 5 Regulations Section 55003: Policies on prerequisites, corequisites, and advisories on recommended preparation* [Appendix B: Title 5, Section 55003, Subsection p(4)]. Retrieved from http://extranet.cccco.edu/Portals/1/AA /Prerequisites/Prerequisites_Guidelines_55003%20Final.pdf

Charles A. Dana Center, Complete College America, Education Commission of the States, Jobs for the Future. (2012). *Core principles for transforming remedial education.* Retrieved from http://www.completecollege.org/docs /Remediation_Joint_Statement-Embargo.pdf

Edgecombe, N., Jaggars, S. S., Xu, D., & Barragan, M. (2014). *Accelerating the integrated instruction of developmental reading and writing at Chabot College.* New York, NY: Community College Research Center, Teachers College, Columbia University.

Fain, P. (2013, October 21). Faster Math Path. *Inside Higher Education.* Retrieved from http://www.insidehighered.com/news/2013/10/21/california-community-colleges -cautious-experiment-accelerated-remediation

Foth, H. (2013, February 21). Faculty reflect on their experience in accelerated classes: Students rise to the occasion [Blog post]. *California Acceleration Project.* Retrieved from http://cap.3csn.org/2013/02/21/faculty-reflect-on-accelerated-classes/

Hayward, C., & Willett, T. (2014). *Curricular redesign and gatekeeper completion: A multi-college evaluation of the California Acceleration Project.* Berkeley, CA: The Research and Planning Group of California Community Colleges. Retrieved from http://cap.3csn.org/files/2014/04/CAPReportFinal3.0.pdf

Hern, K. (with Snell, M.). (2010). Exponential attrition and the promise of acceleration in developmental English and math. *Perspectives.* Berkeley, CA: Research and Planning Group. Retrieved from http://rpgroup.org/sites/default /files/Hern%20Exponential%20Attrition.pdf

Hern, K. (2011). *Accelerated English at Chabot College: A synthesis of key findings.* Hayward, CA: The California Acceleration Project. Retrieved from http://cap.3csn.org/2012/02/24/new-report-chabot-accelerated-english/

Hern, K. (2012). Acceleration across California: Shorter pathways in developmental English and math. *Change: The Magazine of Higher Learning, 44*(3), 60–68. Retrieved from http://cap.3csn.org/files/2011/09/Hern-Acceleration-across-Calif.pdf

Hern, K. (with Snell, M). (2013). *Toward a vision of accelerated curricula and pedagogy: High-challenge, high-support classrooms for underprepared students.* Oakland, CA: LearningWorks. Retrieved from http://www.learningworksca.org /accelerated-pedagogy/

Hetts, J., Fuenmayor, A., & Rothstein, K. (2012). *Promising pathways: Placement, performance, and progress in basic skills and transfer level courses in English and mathematics at Long Beach City College.* Berkeley, CA: The Research and Planning Group. Retrieved from http://www.rpgroup.org/resources/promising-pathways

Jenkins, D., Speroni, C., Belfield, C., Jaggars, D. D., & Edgecombe, N. (2010). *A model for accelerating academic success of community college remedial English students: Is* the *Accelerated Learning Program (ALP) effective and affordable?* (CCRC Working Paper No. 21). New York, NY: Community College Research Center, Teachers College, Columbia University. Retrieved from http://ccrc.tc.columbia.edu/media/k2/attachments/remedial-english-alp-effective-affordable.pdf

Perry, M., Bahr, P. R., Rosin, M., & Woodward, K. M. (2010). *Course-taking patterns, policies, and practices in developmental education in the California community colleges.* Mountain View, CA: EdSource. Retrieved from http://files.eric.ed.gov/fulltext/ED512364.pdf

Scott-Clayton, J. (2012). *Do high-stakes placement exams predict college success?* (CCRC Working Paper No. 41). New York, NY: Community College Research Center, Teachers College, Columbia University. Retrieved from http://ccrc.tc.columbia.edu/media/k2/attachments/high-stakes-predict-success.pdf

KATIE HERN, *EdD, is the director of the California Acceleration Project and an English instructor at Chabot College.*

MYRA SNELL *is the math lead for the California Acceleration Project and a professor of math at Los Medanos College.*

NEW DIRECTIONS FOR COMMUNITY COLLEGES • DOI: 10.1002/cc

4

This chapter defines the integration of academics and student support services and offers examples of models and strategies from colleges nationally.

Strategies for Integrating Student Supports and Academics

Mina Dadgar, Thad Nodine, Kathy Reeves Bracco, Andrea Venezia

Colleges, systems, and states are experimenting with ways to better support student success in community colleges, often with scarce resources and limited staff. Supports offered include academic advising, orientation, assessments, education and career planning, and academic tutoring—in person and via applied technology, depending on the resources at each college. These services can increase students' chances of earning a credential or transferring by providing them additional help to succeed in courses and in navigating college policies and procedures (Bahr, 2008; Weissman et al., 2009), but evidence is growing that the services work best when integrated with what students are learning in the classroom. According to a review of the literature and based on field research at colleges participating in Completion by Design (CBD), a community college initiative funded by the Bill & Melinda Gates Foundation, college efforts to integrate support services with instruction appear to have two overall aims: (a) to expand student access by making services an extension of the classroom and (b) to increase the quality of support services and instruction.

The information used for this chapter is drawn from research materials and from interviews with the following people: Nicholas Bekas, campus dean of Academic Affairs, Valencia College; Jack Friedlander, executive vice president, Educational Programs, Santa Barbara City College; Alison Kadlec, senior vice president, Public Agenda; Zineta Kolenovic, assistant director for Research and Evaluation, Accelerated Study in Associate Programs (ASAP), City University of New York (CUNY); Donna Linderman, university executive director, ASAP, CUNY; Laura Hope, dean, Instructional Support, Chaffey College; Melinda Karp, senior research associate, Community College Research Center, Teachers College, Columbia University; Rob Johnstone, senior research fellow, The Research and Planning Group, California Community Colleges; and Joyce Romano, vice president of Student Affairs, Valencia College.

NEW DIRECTIONS FOR COMMUNITY COLLEGES, no. 167, Fall 2014 © 2014 Wiley Periodicals, Inc.
Published online in Wiley Online Library (wileyonlinelibrary.com) • DOI: 10.1002/cc.20109

Why Integrate Support Services and Instruction?

It makes sense that what we learn and the supports we often need to help us improve our learning—academic advising, orientation, assessments, educational and career planning, and academic tutoring—should be integrated. Most community colleges, however, have organized their instructional functions and student academic supports as separate administrative units, with different personnel groupings, delivery locations, reporting requirements, data systems, and expectations for student participation. This separation of instruction and student supports may help colleges organize their services in more streamlined ways, but it can create obstacles for students if they do not know what kind of supports they need to access in order to succeed in their courses (Nodine, Jaeger, Venezia, & Bracco, 2012; Weissman et al., 2009).

There is growing evidence that integrating those services serves students better. When services are optional and are not offered as part of students' day-to-day college experiences, many students, especially low-income and first-generation students who tend to need the services the most, do not access them (Cox, 2009; Karp, O'Gara, & Hughes, 2008). Extensive interviews with community college students have shown that even with support services open to all students, it is the students with preexisting college know-how who tend to take advantage of them (Karp et al., 2008). In addition, students have indicated that they would like to see greater connections between support services and classroom content (Nodine et al., 2012).

The integration of student support services and instruction takes many forms and might best be considered as a process along a continuum. At one end of the continuum is a highly integrated model, where student services functions are embedded in the academic classroom. At the other end of the continuum are initial efforts at integration, such as professional development for faculty members to learn about the various student services supports offered by the college and how to encourage their students to take advantage of them.

In a highly integrated model, tutoring sessions may be a required component of basic skills classes and may occur during class time. Other examples include the integration of career and educational planning, or supporting the development of study skills during class discussions and assignments. Even when it is not possible to provide support services as part of classroom instruction, there are ways to improve collaboration and alignment between instruction and support services. For example, faculty can require students to receive academic tutoring, encourage students to meet with an advisor, and provide students with reminders of deadlines for registration. Faculty members can also require students to attend staff-led workshops to build study skills. Colleges can support high levels of integration by promoting such concepts as shared goals for student success across campus functions, agreement on strategies for integrating key aspects of student supports and instruction, professional development opportunities that extend outside narrow campus duties, and processes that support ongoing problem solving and dialogue between instructional and student support personnel.

Recently, some community colleges have been working to integrate their instruction and academic support functions to provide a one-stop diagnostic approach that identifies the tutoring or other supports that students need, and then connects them with those services (Dadgar, Nodine, Bracco, & Venezia, 2013). Based on the experiences of these community colleges, it appears that integrating student services more closely with instruction may help to:

- expand student access to supports by making them part of the classroom experience;
- track student progression in real time and help students get back on track if there is a problem;
- encourage students to draw on peer support and other resources;
- engage students more effectively in learning by offering coordinated services;
- address students' needs for support beyond the first year; and
- remove the stigma associated with accessing support by making it integral to the classroom experience of all students.

In this chapter, we synthesize research on how the integration of student support services and instruction may help to support student success, and highlight the strategies that have been implemented nationally. Since this is a newly emerging area of research and practice, there is not a deep base of literature from which to draw upon. For that reason, we also provide information based on interviews with national experts and practitioners. We conclude by examining implementation challenges and opportunities from practitioners' perspectives, and by providing recommendations.

Strategies

Models for integration of instruction and student supports can be characterized in four broad (often overlapping) categories: (a) embedding support in departments and classes, (b) offering integrated student success centers, (c) developing first-year experiences, and (d) using technology to connect student supports and instruction.

Embedding Supports.   Some institutions are embedding student supports in departments or classrooms, thus creating a direct and purposeful connection between student services and instruction and expanding the services to more students. Examples of how this process occurs include designating specific advisors to work with a single or limited number of programs, creating curricular efforts in which faculty and advisors coteach some aspects of the curriculum, and utilizing tutors.

Embedding Advisors in Departments.   Redesigning advising systems to assign advisors to specific departments allows advisors and faculty within a given department to become better acquainted with each other, helps advisors become more familiar with the requirements of that program, and helps faculty learn about advising programs and services. Faculty can provide information to advisors about academic requirements and expectations, and can direct their students to those advisors for support. In addition, this allows students to have some consistency in the advisors they see, at least once they have chosen a program of study. For example, Valencia College used Perkins funds to hire advisors who are embedded in specific career/technical education programs and provide specialized advising to the students in that program. At Tacoma Community College, advisors are designated to areas of concentration such as business, liberal arts, and sciences, and they specialize in advising students in those broad topic areas.

Embedding Advisors in Classrooms.   In some cases, incorporating advisors into courses can be done via "paired" classes in which a cohort of students enrolls in a student success course taught by one teacher, and a math or English course taught by a second teacher, and the two work together to meet students' needs holistically. Another example is where career advisors are brought into classrooms to help students understand careers that might be available to them upon completion of their program. These advisors may also help with incorporating directly into the courses some of the important life skills and habits of mind that students ultimately need in the world of work. According to Jack Friedlander, the executive vice president of Santa Barbara City College, this second model is used in three foundational courses at his college. Student services representatives come directly to these courses to work with students on education and career planning. The instructors and advisors work together to ensure that students learn about career opportunities in the social sciences, business, and science fields, and discuss how jobs in these fields differ.

Embedding Tutors in Classrooms.   To ensure that students receive tutoring support in classes that have a history of low pass rates, some colleges either embed tutors in these high-risk classes, or designate time for meeting with tutors outside of the classroom. In either case, tutors work closely with classroom instructors to ensure that the work they do with the students individually is highly coordinated with the learning goals of the class. Rob Johnstone, formerly of the Research and Planning Group of the California Community Colleges, notes that in some developmental education and introductory courses, scheduling meetings with tutors is part of required class time. This ensures that all students meet with tutors weekly. The format can differ from college to college. For example, some colleges dedicate class time to a tutor who works with students on completing class

NEW DIRECTIONS FOR COMMUNITY COLLEGES • DOI: 10.1002/cc

assignments. Other colleges require students to meet with tutors outside of class but during specific times that are allotted to the class.

Offering Integrated Student Success Centers.   Student success centers are being used by colleges as a model to provide all students, not just a small subset, with a coordinated range of supports. The services provided by the centers are integrated with classroom instruction, are often jointly developed by instructional faculty and success center staff, and can be required of all students in a class. The centers, which are sometimes linked to specific fields (such as humanities or STEM), can house dedicated academic and career counseling, leadership development programs, and student organizations. They can support service learning and community engagement. They can also provide a place where faculty and staff interact informally and formally with students (Collins, 2004).

Laura Hope, the dean of Instructional Support at Chaffey College, notes that student success centers can be particularly effective when they are perceived as a service that everyone uses, not just those who are struggling academically. The success centers at Chaffey are organized by topic and not around developmental education needs, thus eliminating some of the stigma around seeking help at the centers. Hope states, "When everyone is required to seek help, it takes the stigma off. Help-seeking is culturally supported. We wanted to get across that this is not where the failing students go but where successful students go. Students don't keep coming back because they have to ... (but) it has to be a good product for students to come back." According to Hope, the success centers provide a risk-free environment for students to ask questions of staff who will not be grading them in their courses. In a validation of this approach, student surveys at Chaffey show that 98% see a connection between what goes on in the classroom and what happens in the success center.

Developing First-Year Experiences.   Although students need support during their entire college experience, the first year is an especially important time to build their capacity to learn how to navigate both the academic and nonacademic challenges of college. First-year experiences such as orientation and student success courses, when of high quality and coordinated well across academic and support functions, can offer that kind of support. Orientation is becoming increasingly mandatory at community colleges given the importance of developing college know-how among students with the least amount of social capital. Research, however, points to the importance of sustained services beyond the first semester or even the first year (Research Overview, Community College Research Center, 2013).

Most colleges offer student success courses during the first semester or the first year of college. These courses are a relatively inexpensive method for providing advising, education and career planning, and study skills. They also can provide a learning community in which students can get to know and support each other. However, while correlational studies found a positive relationship between participation in these courses and greater persistence and credit accumulation (Cho & Karp, 2012), more rigorous studies found that the effect of the courses faded after a few semesters (Research Overview, Community College Research Center, 2013). In a recent study of student success courses (College 101) in Virginia, the Community College Research Center found that integration is a critical aspect to the success of these courses, and that "explicitly relating" the content of these courses to traditional courses can "increase the likelihood that students find course content useful and know when to access and apply it" (Karp et al., 2008, p. 45).

Another area in which collaboration between the instructional and support functions can improve students' initial experience at community colleges is the assessment and placement process. At most community colleges, incoming students are assessed to determine placement in credit-bearing or non-credit-bearing developmental education courses; this is typically students' first experience with the college. Traditionally, it has been common for students to take the assessments without knowing much about them or having an opportunity to prepare for them (Venezia, Bracco, & Nodine, 2010). Furthermore, in most colleges, assessment and placement is the responsibility of the student services department, and faculty who teach the developmental courses often have little, if any, input in the process. At Valencia College, however, the developmental education faculty members were invited to provide input into the assessment and placement process. As a result, the faculty developed online resources to help students prepare for the tests, and the college recommends new students review these materials prior to the assessment process. Students who are dissatisfied with their placement results can participate in a tutorial and retest once prior to the start of classes.

Using Technology to Connect Student Supports and Instruction. Despite the recent proliferation in the use of technology to provide support services to more students at lower costs, there is little known about the effectiveness of using technology for this purpose. Some of the most common uses of technology in providing support services to students include: (a) online orientation, (b) degree planning, (c) interactive student portals, (d) early alert systems, and (e) the use of predictive analytics to offer individualized support to students. There is no single, widely used model for each of those applications.

The practitioners and experts interviewed highlighted the need to build a human infrastructure around technology tools to ensure that students are aware of and know how to effectively use specific tools and online systems. Even when students use online tools, they may still need help in understanding and applying the information they are receiving. For example, while technology-based degree audits can be helpful in allowing students to check their progress toward their degrees/certificates, colleges have found it important to complement the audit tool with in-person advising, especially when students need to discuss their options about changing their major or if they are undecided about their field of study.

Implementation

Strategies to integrate instruction and support services can take a variety of forms. At Santa Barbara City College, long-term collaborations by faculty and staff culminated in organizational restructuring so that faculty and support services staff now report to the same vice president. In other colleges, integration has been achieved without formal changes in organizational structures, but has generally required the creation of common goals, strategies, and decision making across instruction and support services (such as through the development of collaborative student success centers, shared technologies, and joint first-year experience programs). All of the interviewees highlighted the importance of building a culture of collaboration to support these efforts.

It is difficult to assess the effects of integration in isolation, partly because they often occur alongside other efforts to increase completion rates. However, administrators who implemented integration strategies described these efforts as successful in (a) expanding access to support services by making them an extension of the classroom and (b) improving the quality of both classroom instruction and support services by coordinating the two. In addition, interviewees indicated that developing shared strategies and programs, over the long run, had facilitated the work of both faculty and support services staff, partly because each became more aware of the ramifications of their own decisions across campus functions.

A challenge in developing strategies to increase the integration of support services and instructional functions is engaging staff and faculty in the process. Some faculty may be concerned that integration will increase their responsibilities without providing them with adequate recognition, compensation, or professional development. Support services staff may be concerned that integration could lessen the need for professional advisors and other support staff. In addition, interviewees said that in many colleges, the existing channels of communication between instruction and student support functions are very limited, and this has led to a lack of understanding and respect for the work of the other side, which makes engagement efforts more challenging to begin with.

If efforts to create a more integrated experience for students are to be successful, they will likely require some changes in the traditional roles of faculty and staff. Interviewees noted, however, that the changes do not necessarily lead to increased responsibility; even in a more integrated model of advisement, faculty members are not expected to provide "deep advising." Rather, they are expected to be the first point of contact for many students and, as such, to know enough about support services to refer students correctly. Nicholas Bekas of Valencia College said, "We never expect faculty to do deep advising and counseling on behavioral issues or financial aid, but it is mostly about career goals that they can advise.... In reality, if faculty can talk with the students and help them realize students' goals, it will actually help [faculty] in the classroom."

Beyond advising, integration can also lead to changes in how faculty and staff work together to link classroom instruction with career planning, educational planning, and tutoring. In these efforts, support services staff members are able to be more proactive in working with classroom instructors to identify the academic and nonacademic skills that students need in order to succeed in their classes and programs, and to develop the capacity of students to identify when and how to seek help, how to manage their time, and how to navigate college policies and procedures. For example, instructors and support services staff can work together to develop exercises that improve students' academic and nonacademic skills necessary to succeed both in a particular classroom and in the longer term.

Recommendations

The culture of each campus drives the extent to which the integration of academic and student supports is possible. For example, it can be quite threatening to advisors to think about faculty becoming more integrally involved in what is typically in the advisors' hands and vice versa. In some states, the issue of integration could become subject to union negotiations, which may be particularly challenging if counselors and faculty are not represented by the same union. Then, there are more logistical issues related to how academic and student affairs deans, and advisors and faculty, can reasonably share responsibilities on a day-to-day basis. These issues point to the need to take the time to build a culture of collaboration and to offer professional development for both faculty and advisors, and the examples in this chapter provide information about how culture can shift over time. The experiences of interviewees in integrating instruction and support services suggest the importance of the following approaches for engaging faculty and staff.

Consider Starting With Programs in Which There Is a History of Collaboration. Interviewees suggested that colleges seeking to integrate support services and instructional functions consider beginning with programs or strategies for which there is a history of collaboration. In many colleges, for example, instructors of developmental education already have extensive experience helping students develop study skills and connecting students with advising and tutoring services. Similarly, programs that create common first-year experiences for large numbers of incoming students may be able to build on existing faculty–staff collaborations. Using technology to alert advisors about classroom performance has been another natural place of collaboration among faculty and student services staff.

NEW DIRECTIONS FOR COMMUNITY COLLEGES • DOI: 10.1002/cc

At Valencia and Chaffey Colleges, developmental education was at the center of integration efforts because faculty and staff recognized the importance of advising and support services in contributing to student success in developmental education. Nicholas Bekas of Valencia College said, "Our developmental education faculty members are already doing advising because of the needs of the students. The next step is to help them understand that by doing advising they can actually teach more because developmental advising equips students with the tools necessary to be independent learners.... I think you will always have a group of faculty who will not get involved, but you usually start with the willing and build a critical mass."

Strengthen the Campus Culture of Collaboration and Student Success. Interviewees also suggested that college efforts at integration should develop and strengthen the campus culture of collaboration, improvement, and student success. This means that faculty and staff should be included in planning processes early on and continually. For example, Santa Barbara City College and Valencia College included student services staff with faculty on important formal governance structures, including governance councils, the academic senate, and cross-functional workgroups. In addition, informal collaborative spaces have reinforced the formal structures. For example, Valencia College has "reading circles" in which faculty and staff from different functions gather to read and discuss the most recent literature in the field. This, according to Joyce Romano, vice president for Student Affairs, has allowed faculty and staff to "develop shared vocabulary and understanding, and big ideas have emerged from that."

Santa Barbara City College's experience with integration is a success story that highlights the importance of a long-term process to strengthen collaboration. Jack Friedlander, who was the dean for Academic Affairs when the process began, led a gradual yet persistent process of integration that culminated in uniting the instructional and support functions under his supervision. As a first step, he created a Deans' Council that was comprised of student support service staff and instructional deans. The Deans' Council met every other week and discussed strategies to improve student completion. Friedlander believes that the formal structure allowed the two sides to develop an understanding of each other's work, which led to formal recognition of equal status for student support faculty in the Academic Senate, which in turn facilitated the organizational restructuring. According to Friedlander, "having student services faculty be represented [in the academic senate] was a huge structural change that increased understanding, appreciation, and collaboration, and after two years it led to creating instructional programs all integrated under one unit." Currently, most decisions are made by cross-functional work groups. "I call together a group of faculty and student services staff when there is a challenge or opportunity ... Once people started trying it out, it was effortless. I only orchestrate at a high level, because people themselves decided to work collaboratively and over time it got better."

NEW DIRECTIONS FOR COMMUNITY COLLEGES • DOI: 10.1002/cc

Use Professional Development More Effectively As a Step Toward Integrating Services.   Colleges that have successfully integrated instruction and support services provide extensive professional development for both faculty and support services staff. They also provide incentives for full-time and adjunct faculty to participate in the training opportunities. According to interviewees, an important source of concern for many faculty members is that they lack information about and experience in providing advising and other support services for students.

Since efforts to provide a more integrated experience for students affect the traditional roles of faculty and staff, professional development is essential. Professional development can provide information that faculty and support services staff need to understand their roles in supporting student learning not just in their classroom or in their advising session, but also in meeting students' overall goals for completion. It can also help to ensure that service delivery is consistent across departments and that all faculty and staff feel supported in addressing students' nonacademic and academic needs.

Interviewees said that the creation of formal incentives can help to encourage faculty participation in professional development. At Valencia College, faculty members receive training on the various campus services that are available, and adjunct faculty members are given monetary incentives to complete relevant training certifications. The certification consists of required modules that include topics such as how to advise developmental education students and how to promote college success skills. There are also elective courses on topics such as how to motivate students and how to promote student development of affective skills.

In addition, interviewees suggested that consistent and standardized professional development is necessary to improve the quality of the support services provided both by instructional and support services staff. This sentiment is echoed by students who have stated that they are frustrated by receiving different advice depending on which advisor or faculty they approach (Nodine et al., 2012). According to Donna Linderman, the director of the Accelerated Study in Associate Programs for the City University of New York, "Everyone who provides advising should be trained not only in what classes are available but also in how to access different services. . . . Standardized curriculum for training advisors is needed—a curriculum that is based on learning outcomes for advising."

Conclusion

Developing a culture that can support and sustain the integration of student services with instruction may be a necessary part of comprehensive reforms focused on increasing degree and certificate completion. There are several models for integration (from embedding supports in classrooms to training instructors to refer students for assistance), but they all share two overall aims: (a) to make student services and supports a natural part of students' college experience and (b) to increase the quality of both support services and instruction.

References

Bahr, P. R. (2008). Cooling out in the community college: What is the effect of academic advising on students' chances of success? *Research in Higher Education, 49*(8), 704–732.

Cho, S. W., & Karp, M. M. (2012). *Student success courses and educational outcomes at Virginia community colleges* (CCRC Working Paper No. 40). New York, NY: Community College Research Center, Teachers College, Columbia University. Retrieved from http://ccrc.tc.columbia.edu/media/k2/attachments/student-success-course-outcomes-virginia.pdf

Collins, A. G. (2004). *The evolution to academic excellence: Key driver for Clarkson's overall evolution to excellence*. Potsdam, NY: Clarkson University. Retrieved from http://www.clarkson.edu/about/welcome/documents/evolution.pdf

Cox, R. D. (2009). *The college fear factor: How students and professors misunderstand one another*. Cambridge, MA: Harvard University Press.

Dadgar, M., Nodine, T., Bracco, K. R., & Venezia, A. (2013). *Integrating student supports and academics*. San Francisco, CA: WestEd.

Karp, M. M., O'Gara, L., & Hughes, K. L. (2008). *Do support services at community colleges encourage success or reproduce disadvantage? An exploratory study of students in two community colleges* (CCRC Working Paper No. 10). New York, NY: Community College Research Center, Teachers College, Columbia University.

Nodine, T., Jaeger, L., Venezia, A., & Bracco, K. R. (2012). *Connection by design: Students' perceptions of their community college experiences*. San Francisco, CA: WestEd.

Research Overview, Community College Research Center. (2013, September). *What we know about nonacademic student supports*. New York, NY: Community College Research Center, Teachers College, Columbia University.

Venezia, A., Bracco, K. R., & Nodine, T. (2010). *One-shot deal? Students' perceptions of assessment and course placement in California's community colleges*. San Francisco, CA: WestEd.

Weissman, E., Cerna, O., Geckeler, C., Schneider, E., Price, D. V., & Smith, T. J. (2009). *Promoting partnerships for student success: Lessons from the SSPIRE initiative*. New York, NY: MDRC. Retrieved from http://www.mdrc.org/publications/521/overview.html

MINA DADGAR *is the director of research for the Career Ladders Project.*

THAD NODINE *is a novelist and a writer of education policy.*

KATHY REEVES BRACCO *is a senior research associate at WestEd.*

ANDREA VENEZIA *is an associate professor of public policy and administration and the executive director of the Institute for Higher Education Leadership & Policy at California State University, Sacramento.*

5

This chapter describes the University of Hawaii's work to develop an online navigational tool that helps students develop and execute their educational plans, and assists colleges with ensuring that they have the capacity to meet students' needs.

Providing Transparent Information to Empower Students' Decision Making and Develop Institutional Capacity

Gary Rodwell

History and Context

Over the past 5–10 years, community college budgets have been slashed in states across the country. Matriculation services—the point of entry for new and prospective students—have been gutted in many colleges, making already tough advisor/student ratios even worse. Amid these changes, different forms of technology are being used to see if they can provide low-cost, large-scale alternatives to help students be more connected to their colleges, navigate within and across student services and academics, and track their progress.

Many college students, particularly those in community colleges, do not know how to choose the most appropriate major, nor do they know how to put together a sequence of courses that allows for both exploration and focus. This can be particularly challenging in open access institutions such as community colleges with large pressures to graduate students in two to four years and very few advising resources. Community colleges are testing advising-related possibilities with technology, balancing high student needs with opportunities to effectively provide "low touch" information to large numbers of students.

This chapter presents information on a new technology system developed over the past eight years at the University of Hawaii (UH) and used by community colleges in Hawaii as well called an "Academic Pathway System" (APS). APS helps students navigate the tension between exploring curricular options and committing to a program of study or major, while at the same time creating a system of checks and balances for the institution itself.

New Directions for Community Colleges, no. 167, Fall 2014 © 2014 Wiley Periodicals, Inc.
Published online in Wiley Online Library (wileyonlinelibrary.com) • DOI: 10.1002/cc.20110

By uploading information about students' plans, it helps institutions plan and commit to providing the resources necessary for the degree pathways demanded. The initial resources to start the APS came from the reallocation of two personnel who were working on the UH's Degree Audit system.

The reasons for the development of the APS were threefold:

1. Create transparency between institutions and their students so that students and advisors become partners together in creating degree pathways and tools to help student stay on-track.
2. Unite all of the 10 public postsecondary institutions and their 60,000 students in Hawaii (seven community colleges and three four-year institutions), so that seamless degree pathways could be created utilizing courses from any UH institution.
3. Feed all the student degree pathway data back to the programs offering the degrees so the programs can analyze, understand, and overcome the constraints that are restricting their throughput (such as a lack of seats in core courses or overly complex degree requirements).

An initial driver of the APS was that the University of Hawaii's leadership acknowledged that there was a significant breakdown in the engagement between the institution and students along each student's pathway. Such a breakdown was creating a situation in which not enough students were graduating and many who were graduating were not attached enough to their institutions to become active alumni and stewards of their alma maters. An example was a student who was receiving accolades from the dean of her college for making the dean's list for four consecutive semesters. However, it became apparent that even though the student had a 4.0 GPA and was taking 14 credits a semester she had been taking courses unrelated to her degree program and was not progressing to completion at an acceptable rate and would run out of financial aid before completing her degree program.

A more systemic example occurred during the development of a new associate degree program at a community college in Hawaii. The associate degree was made of many different disciplines and each discipline's faculty members were passionate about the importance of their discipline to the degree program as a whole. The result was a "grand compromise" between all the disciplines that led to the development of *overly complex* degree requirements and choices, just to ensure all disciplines and individuals within each academic unit's interests were represented in the newly created degree program. The APS system was one of the major initiatives put forth eight years ago to help address both individual and systemic level problems such as these.

The administration at the time noticed that, regardless of the problem, it becomes the responsibility of the student to overcome it, often with little to no contact with a person who has deep knowledge about the issue(s).

NEW DIRECTIONS FOR COMMUNITY COLLEGES • DOI: 10.1002/cc

This forces the students to become "masters" of the requirement structures, or face possible costly mistakes and slower progress toward completion. An APS system can play a key role in the identification of programs with, for example, overly complex degree requirements.

What Is APS?

When students are asked what the APS is (which is known as "STAR" on the UH campuses), they usually respond with a statement such as, "It's a web app like Facebook except it lets me see how I have done over time toward my degree, what I need to do next, and when I'm going to graduate at UH at any of the campuses." For educators and administrators, the answer tends to be more complex since they know that the APS feeds back information about possible degree program constraints that may hinder students from staying on track. It is then an institutional responsibility to remove or reduce those constraints.

Most succinctly, an APS system is the next generation of what is currently called "degree audit software." Degree audit software are usually akin to a computer system that enables students to review academic coursework to evaluate which degree requirements are complete and which degree requirements are remaining, in a report type format. The APS has the following additional constructs on top of a baseline degree audit system:

1. Spans multiple institutions.
2. Illustrates a student's academic progress in a web portal, including every moment in time choices that led up to those moments, where he/she currently stands, and when he/she is likely to graduate.
3. Maps out a "best" academic pathway forward per student, semester by semester to graduation and adapts as the student deviates from her/his initial plans.
4. Creates alerts (both positive and negative) when a student changes the "velocity toward completion" of his/her degree program.
5. Collectively uses the all students' changes in degree program "velocity toward completion" over time to identify systemic issues in a degree program.

These five features are described in more detail below.

Spanning Multiple Institutions.   An APS ideally spans multiple institutions since it allows students to make comparisons easily across campuses and take courses between campuses seamlessly. For example, a student can register for a course at any institution in the UH system, and in real time the APS will reflect the corresponding transfer articulated course in the student's home institution and how it meets the student's degree program requirements.

New Directions for Community Colleges • DOI: 10.1002/cc

While it is critical that institutions have articulation systems in place at all the campuses for this to work, it is not critical that the systems are comprehensively populated with all equivalencies since the APS has built-in triggers that notify the institution(s) when the articulation equivalences are missing. For example, when a student registers for a course at another UH institution that does not articulate back to the student's home institution, the student's home institution's registrar receives an alert that (a) lets them know one of their students is taking a course at another institution that has no transfer articulation equivalent and (b) asks the registrar if it would like to create an equivalent course.

This same boundary spanning capability has opened a plethora of other opportunities like an automatic reverse transfer process and automatic degree conferral. Holly Zanville, senior research officer at Lumina Foundation for Education, stated, "Hawaii may be the furthest ahead in statewide coordination [with regard to reverse transfer]" (Fain, 2012, para. 8).

Academic Progress Narrative.   At the core of the APS is the ability to illustrate a student's academic progress at every moment in time, how he/she got there, where he/she currently is, and when he/she is likely to graduate. Figure 5.1 is an example "academic progress narrative" that is generated in real time and viewable on the APS web interface (available to both the advisor and student). This is just one of the components on the APS interface and it is designed to be an overview of how the student is progressing toward their degree requirements overtime.

Figure 5.1 is an illustration of a student's "academic progress narrative." In this example, the student starts at a community college and has an almost perfect rate of completion ("velocity toward completion") of degree requirements, graduating with an associate degree in five semesters in spring 2009, which implies a rate of completion of approximately 20% of his degree requirements per semester (this can be seen by the slope of the first line in the graph).

The student then moves straight on to a four-year UH campus after graduating from the community college and pursues a bachelor's degree in English and has a great "velocity toward completion" of degree requirements up until fall 2010. After that the student's "velocity toward completion" decreases to almost zero. The student is still taking 15 credits a semester (five classes), however, only one of the classes he is taking counts toward his major's degree requirements (even though the student is receiving A's in his classes). This persists for four semesters until the student changes majors and loses more than a year's worth of work and classes. The student is now predicted to graduate in his new major in three more semesters (spring 2014).

The "academic progress narrative" in Figure 5.1 was able to illustrate another systemic failure. This student completed an associate degree, but entered the four-year institution with only 40% of his four-year degree requirements complete. The associate degree should represent 50% of the

Figure 5.1. Academic Progress Narrative

My University of Hawaiʻi Academic Progress Narrative

Manoa Undergraduate Arts & Sci BA/ENG (Primary) Fall 2009, 89.67%

Graduated

Kapiolani CC Undergraduate Arts & Sciences AA/LBRT (Primary) Fall 2008, 61.00%

Predicted Graduation

Changed Major

Re-Enrolled

Legend

--- Predicted pathway

— Student enrolled

● Point of graduation

A University of Hawaii Venture

student's four-year degree program (in terms of degree requirement); if that is not the case, that means that a percentage of the student's associate degree program is not being counted toward his four-year program requirements. Therefore, the student lost 10% of his degree requirements or one semester's worth of work in the transition to the four-year campus. The solution is simple from a very broad perspective: If a student would like to transfer to a four-year campus from a community college, she should have a clear map or transfer pathway to follow to her intended major.

Mapping Out a "Best" Academic Pathway. The next construct of the APS is the "best academic pathway forward." No matter where a student is in his degree program, the APS needs to be able to map out the student's best path forward to graduation regardless of whether the student is an incoming first-year student, a transfer student, a part-time student, a full-time student, etc. Hence, no matter where the student is in his or her degree program or which requirements the student has already completed, the APS will be able to identify the best path forward semester by semester to graduation. The easiest comparison to existing technologies is the GPS that keeps recalculating your path even if you take detours.

As Figure 5.2 shows, the student's entire path forward is mapped out, and the APS can be configured to run for part-time students, full-time students, and so forth with a drop and drag interface.

Using the Data to Create Alerts. In an APS system, the rate of completion over time is of central importance; this is what we have termed the

Figure 5.2. Example Academic Plan

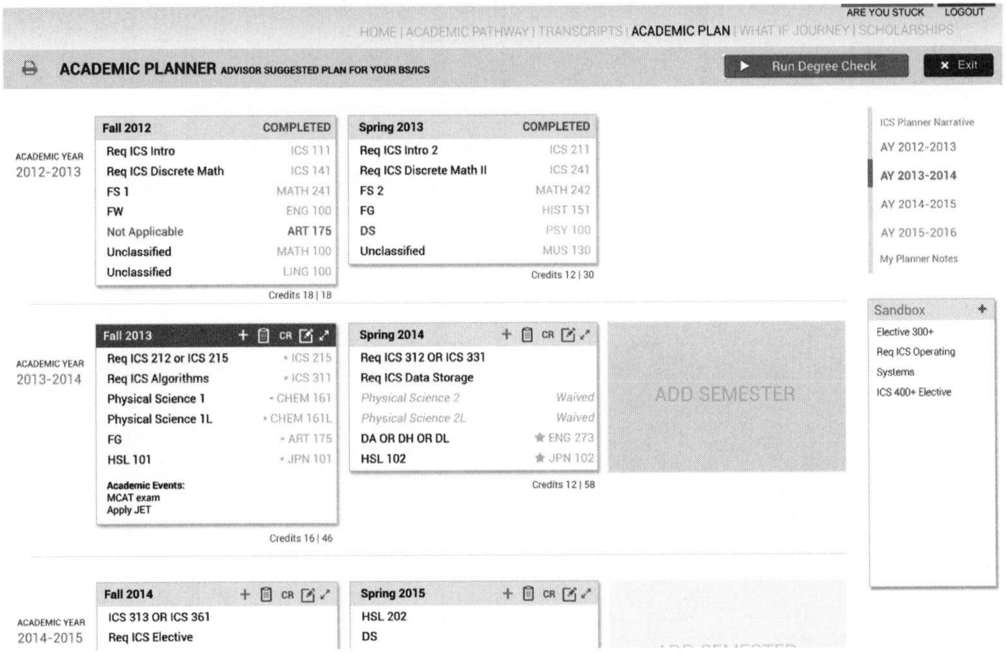

•
•
•
•

"student velocity toward completion" of degree program requirements or just "velocity." For example, for a student to graduate in two years with an associate degree, she should ideally complete 25% of the requirements each semester in order to be 100% complete with the degree requirements (assuming there are two semesters in an academic year). Hence "velocity" is based on the rate at which a student completes degree requirements. It is the rate of change of the velocity (acceleration and deceleration) that we are most interested in as it alerts us to potential issues. If, for example, a student is going at a rate of 25% a semester for three semesters then suddenly drops to 10%, the APS raises an alert before the end of the registration period so the student has the ability to change his or her course choices.

Using the Aggregate "Velocity" Data to Identify Systemic Degree Program Challenges.   The velocity over time of all students' academic pathways combined can be employed collectively to identify systemic issues within a degree program. Each student has an academic pathway graph; behind each graph for each student are the data that creates the graph. These same data that can create the individuals' graphs can be used at an aggregate level to identify systemic challenges for specific academic programs.

There is significant debate nationally on how to measure an academic program or department's efficiency, in that a unit may be seen in negative light if its students graduate at a slower pace on average or with significantly more credits then the program requires. However, from the department's perspective, students may have transferred into its degree program with a significant amount of credits, and hence the department is not responsible for students' excessive credits at graduation. This becomes even more complex when students transfer in from other institutions, which is why postsecondary education graduation efficiency benchmarks generally take only first-time incoming students into consideration and not transfer students when determining student success statistics.

Looking at the question of program throughput efficiency from APS perspective, the answer is simple. To measure a unit's efficiency at keeping its students on track just look the "average student body velocity" (sum up the velocities of all the students in that program for that semester and divide by the number of students in the program). This will eliminate the number of credits with which students entered into the program; it is only the average velocity of all students once they have entered your program. Hence, if the statistics point toward a slower-than-normal average student velocity in a particular degree program, this may indicate systemic issues within the program. Programs can hone in on potential problems by, for example, determining which year(s) slowdowns most often occur (first, second, third, etc.). In addition, this measure can be supplemented with the "rate of change in student body velocity" upon entering the program. By comparing average student velocity prior to coming into the program with student velocity once in the program, we can again identify if there are any systemic issues. These two new department/program throughput efficiency markers

Figure 5.3.   Post-APS Implementation Data: Hawaii Community College Total Completions

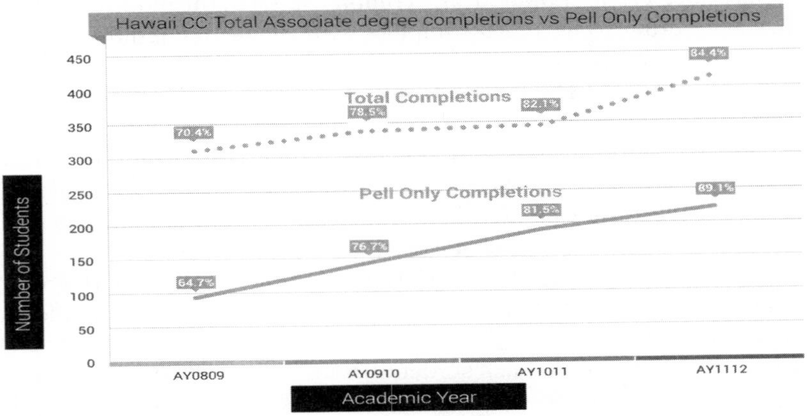

are the hallmarks of an APS and will take significant time to implement. The markers are being rolled out in spring 2014 for the UH.

Performance of the APS

UH went live with our APS system six years ago; currently there are 1.6 million logins a year. Over these six years, we have seen a significant increase in completion numbers (for both Pell eligible and non-Pell eligible students) at individual institutions (as can be seen in the example of Hawaii Community College in Figure 5.3) and across the UH system as a whole. Across the system, completions of degrees and certificates awarded by all the campuses in the UH system went from 8,988 in 2010–2011 to 9,628 in 2011–2012—an increase of 7.1%. In the long term, these trends will accelerate as a new Automatic Reverse Transfer process is expected to yield 700 more degrees per semester and the automatic conferral of certificates will yield another 500 certificates a semester. As Figure 5.3 shows, total completions each year increased from 70.4% (2009) to 78.5% (2010) to 82.1% (2011) to 84.4% (2012). Over those same years, Pell completions increased from 64.7% to 76.7% to 81.5% to 89.1%.

The Technology

The APS system "STAR" was designed to interface with any base student information systems, such as PeopleSoft, Datatel, or Banner via an Application Programing Interface. However, this has not been verified since all the institutions of public postsecondary education in the state of Hawaii are on a Banner (Ellucian Higher Education) system. As the APS construct

NEW DIRECTIONS FOR COMMUNITY COLLEGES • DOI: 10.1002/cc

gathers momentum, there are compelling arguments to move STAR into an Open Source Software model; however at this point that has yet to be decided since it would require dedication of significant resources. Our current staffing model for development and maintenance is an interface programmer, a back-end programmer, an architect, a handful of very talented student employees, two grant-funded hires, and a student support specialist that is the glue for the unit.

Conclusion

While higher education tops most agendas, there is a deep legislative division nationwide about whether the main problem is a lack of money or if there are problems with the education enterprise (such as governance, etc.). An APS has the capacity to get at the core of the efficiency question and ensure that there are checks and balances.

In the next five to ten years, the largest constraint to the adoption of APS systems nationwide is likely less related to the availability of technology and more about the political capital necessary to form alliances among institutions within each state. Creating such alliances would take a big step toward ensuring that students can move seamlessly on clear supported pathways, and that institutions and programs accept responsibility when students, on average, cannot stay on track in their programs.

Reference

Fain, P. (2012, May 23). Common sense on completion. *Inside Higher Ed.* Retrieved from http://www.insidehighered.com/news/2012/05/23/statewide-reverse-transfer-catches-could-boost-graduation-rates

GARY RODWELL *is an information technology specialist with UH Manoa's Office of Undergraduate Education.*

6

This chapter reports on a major college-wide effort to smooth students' paths as they enter the college, choose a program, and progress to a credential. Leadership, inclusiveness, and communication have been central to the success of the effort.

Strengthening Program Pathways Through Transformative Change

Lenore Rodicio, Susan Mayer, Davis Jenkins

Beginning in 2005, Miami Dade College (MDC) began a process of defining the skills students would need to thrive in the 21st century. In 2007, the faculty and student body signed a covenant "to build a foundation for the success of future students," codifying 10 learning outcomes that degree program graduates would be expected to master to prepare them to be effective employees, engaged citizens, and lifelong learners (Padrón, 2009, para. 1). Since then, the college has organized a semiannual, college-wide assessment process to see how well students are achieving these outcomes. Faculty use the results to identify areas where students need to improve their skills—and thus where instruction needs to be strengthened. Faculty in each discipline have mapped the curriculum to discern how each course introduces or reinforces relevant goals. Faculty are encouraged to develop course-specific assessments, and this has been facilitated through training and professional development.

While this process has helped to ensure that learning goals are aligned across the curriculum in every degree program and that advancing students are in fact acquiring essential competencies, the college also found that too many students were not completing programs. In examining why many students do not complete programs, the college found that the curriculum in each program was not necessarily coherent to students. Students had too many course choices and too little guidance in selecting a path toward completion, and they needed more help in developing their goals for further education and employment. Academic support was often misaligned with academic programs, and the information students received to help them navigate academic programs and support services was often unclear and inconsistent. These realizations provided the impetus for a comprehensive,

New Directions for Community Colleges, no. 167, Fall 2014 © 2014 Wiley Periodicals, Inc.
Published online in Wiley Online Library (wileyonlinelibrary.com) • DOI: 10.1002/cc.20111

college-wide effort to redesign programs and supports in ways that help students more easily navigate college and achieve their goals.

In 2011, the college launched a major new initiative to strengthen pathways to degree completion, facilitate transfer to baccalaureate programs, and support students' advancement in the labor market. From the outset, MDC's goal has been transformative change. Small-scale, incremental improvements would not be adequate to produce the improvements in student outcomes the college was seeking. College leaders recognized that big changes could be achieved only through broadly inclusive engagement of faculty and staff "from the bottom up" in a process of inquiry, problem solving, and results-oriented action. Two-and-a-half years into the reforms, MDC has successfully engaged faculty and staff in mapping out curriculum pathways in the largest program areas of the colleges, creating seamless "on-ramps" to help new students choose and enter programs of study in these fields, and improving ongoing support services to facilitate student progression along the pathways. While MDC is still working to strengthen degree pathways, this chapter describes how one of the largest higher education institutions in the country set in motion reforms that have in a short timeframe produced big changes in practice that we believe will lead to substantial improvements in student outcomes.

Setting Big Changes in Motion

In August 2011, the college kicked off the initiative, embarking on a yearlong planning process with three objectives: (a) cultivate a collective understanding of the scope of the problems students encounter as they navigate through the college; (b) create a comprehensive plan to address the problems; and (c) build support for the initiative, particularly among faculty, staff, and administrators who did not participate directly in the planning. More than 120 faculty, staff, and administrators were tasked with analyzing college data on student progression patterns to identify barriers to success and examine the root causes of these barriers. Initially, the planning teams were organized by each of the college's eight campuses, but after these teams shared their findings on barriers to student success at a college-wide retreat, the teams realized that the campuses had more similarities than differences, and the planning teams were restructured into integrated, college-wide teams.

After extensive analysis and deliberation, the teams recommended changes to curriculum, pedagogy, and student support and administrative services needed to facilitate student progression and success. As part of the process, the findings and recommendations were shared and debated among faculty and staff across the campuses in multiple venues. Initiative leaders tried to frame the findings in terms that would be compelling to college faculty and others. For example, to demonstrate the need to strengthen program pathways, data were presented on the numbers of associate degree

New Directions for Community Colleges • DOI: 10.1002/cc

graduates who earn credits in excess of the required number, and on the cost to students of earning these excess credits.

This yearlong planning and engagement process resulted in a set of recommendations for improving student outcomes including the following:

- *Develop structured program pathways* that clearly lead to transfer and career outcomes. Courses and course sequences should be aligned with the college's learning outcome goals and with the requirements for junior standing in baccalaureate programs at MDC and its partner universities.
- *Create a comprehensive intake process* that includes mandatory orientation, assigned advisors, and holistic assessments of student motivation and metacognitive skills. The intake process should be designed to increase students' early engagement with the college and help them choose and enter a program of study as soon as possible.
- *Integrate academic programs and student support services* to improve student persistence and completion. The planning teams recommended a new, intrusive coaching and mentoring model to help students make steady progress on their program pathways. Students would receive advising, coaching, and mentoring from the time they were admitted to the college until they graduate through a partnership between student services and academic departments, which would use enhanced student information and academic planning technology systems to monitor student progress.
- *Strengthen students' transition from developmental education and English language learner programs* into college-level programs of study by redesigning and expanding contextualized, accelerated, and modularized course offerings and linking them to diagnostic information about individual student skill gaps and needs. Developmental education programs had been streamlined recently; the planning team recommended also streamlining the English as a Second Language for Academic Purposes program, introducing college-level coursework earlier in the sequence, and contextualizing instruction in foundation skills to the student's field of interest.
- *Increase student engagement through communities of interest.* Entering students would choose a broad program area or "community of interest" based on their educational and career goals. Communities of interest would provide additional opportunities for students to benefit from academic, extracurricular, and career activities related to their field of interest, and they would allow students to engage with a community of other students and faculty with common interests.

The college-wide teams were reconstituted as integrated implementation teams and charged with developing detailed execution plans for each of the five recommendations listed. Although work began on all five areas, the teams recommended prioritizing the initial implementation work on the first three, since mapping program pathways, redesigning the intake process, and integrating support services would be essential to efforts to accelerate underprepared students' transition to college-level programs and to building communities of interest.

Strengthening Program Pathways

To strengthen program pathways, MDC formed the Undergraduate Pathways Planning Group (UPP), which was made up of 27 faculty members representing each of the schools and major disciplines at the college. The UPP team decided to focus initially on mapping pathways in four target disciplines—business, psychology, biology, and criminal justice—that are among the college's largest programs, accounting for nearly 80% of the college's students. Faculty in each of these disciplines were supported by other UPP members in the general education disciplines. This collaboration helped to facilitate cross-discipline thinking and learning, which is essential for creating coherent programs of study.

Identifying which courses would be recommended for inclusion in each program pathway was a potentially contentious task, since it meant that some courses would be excluded. And some faculty wondered why it was necessary to create more structured pathways, expressing the view that students should be able and encouraged to explore different subject areas on their own.

Thus, in fall 2012, UPP faculty participated in a series of exercises designed to help them build the skills needed to facilitate conversations about program pathways, both within their own disciplines and across departments. In one memorable exercise, the UPP faculty were given the transcript of a student who was currently enrolled at MDC and seeking to transfer to a local university and pursue a bachelor's degree in biology; UPP faculty were asked to help the student determine the most appropriate courses to choose to complete the second year of his studies so that he would be able to transfer with junior status in his field. The UPP members could not figure out from the existing discipline program sheets the prerequisites required by the transfer institution or the specific courses that would transfer. The task was made even more complicated by the addition of information about state prerequisite requirements. One faculty member said half-jokingly, "I think I'll recommend that the student major in English, because I can figure that path out." This experience helped to galvanize support among the team members for more clearly structured program pathways, and UPP team members became champions for the pathway redesign work.

Each of the pathway teams mapped out a pathway for full-time students (enrolled in 12 or more credits) and one for part-time students (enrolled in at least six credits) that included curriculum "on-ramps" for students who start in developmental and English-as-a-Second-Language programs. In mapping out the program pathways, the UPP was encouraged to start with students' end goals in mind. The team agreed on uniform design guidelines for the program pathways, stipulating that each pathway provide adequate coverage of MDC's 10 learning outcome goals for degree programs so that graduates would have the core skills and knowledge needed for further education and employment.

In addition, all courses in each pathway should transfer seamlessly to enable students to achieve junior standing in bachelor's programs with minimal loss of credits. To this end, the teams incorporated Florida's general education prerequisites into the pathways, along with the courses required for related bachelor's degree programs offered by the college and by Florida International University (FIU), the destination institution for over half of MDC students who transfer. They were aided in this by FIU's MyMajor website, which provides in-depth information about all FIU undergraduate majors, including admissions criteria, career opportunities, and the departments' contact information. The team also benefitted from the strong working relationship that MDC has with FIU. Each year, administrators from the two institutions meet to discuss their priorities for the year. One of MDC's key priorities when the two institutions met in March 2012 was the mapping out of more structured and aligned associate degree pathways that would enable transfer students from MDC to start their junior year on equal footing with native FIU students.

The pathway design teams were also asked to identify the specific general education courses that were most relevant to and preparatory for each program pathway. For example, the criminal justice pathway might indicate, "This is the social science course recommended for the criminal justice pathway." In other pathway areas, students have more flexibility to choose electives. For instance, the biology pathway has a prescribed sequence of science and math courses but allows students to choose from a broad range of arts and humanities courses for their electives. Throughout the pathway design process, the college's institutional research staff provided analysis to support the UPP's decision making. For example, business faculty hypothesized that students who enrolled in business statistics without having completed any math courses higher than intermediate algebra would not perform well in the statistics course. When the data were analyzed, however, the business faculty learned that students who entered business statistics by way of intermediate algebra performed as well as students who placed directly into statistics.

The UPP members were responsible for vetting drafts of pathway maps with their respective departments and for communicating feedback back to the UPP team. In general, the conversations about which courses to include or not include in the various pathways went surprisingly smoothly. Great effort was made to include in these discussions everyone who wanted to participate—including those who were skeptical about the need to map pathways. These deliberations produced a rich diversity of ideas and feedback, which not only helped to facilitate the process but also strengthened the pathway maps themselves.

The most difficult conversations occurred in relation to the psychology pathway, which compared with the other fields has the least-defined requirements at both the associate and bachelor's levels. Additional support was provided to the psychology department through a retreat, which gave the faculty time and facilitated support to discuss the issues that had emerged during the pathway mapping process. Full participation was encouraged and all issues—"the good, the bad, and the ugly"—were discussed. While the conversations were difficult and sometimes emotional, the faculty came together to create a pathway that now has their ownership and support.

Overall, more than 200 faculty members were engaged in the pathway redesign process. The UPP submitted drafts of the pathways to the student services directors, the Implementation Council (the initiative's steering committee), and the academic deans, who provided feedback. The pathways were presented to the College Academic and Student Support Council, which reviews and helps to disseminate new and revised curricula across the college, and they were implemented in fall 2013 term.

Building Better On-Ramps to Programs of Study

While the UPP was beginning its work mapping out program pathways, MDC launched an effort to restructure its new student intake experience to provide the information, advising, and support students need to choose and successfully enter a program path. Initial implementation of the redesigned intake process targeted the cohort of approximately 9,000 students entering MDC directly from high school in fall 2012. The changes included disallowing late registration; augmenting the number and scope of "mini-term" courses for students who missed registration deadlines; establishing uniform, mandatory orientations for new students that incorporated noncognitive diagnostic assessments and course registration; assigning advisors to incoming students; and offering "boot camps" for students requiring remediation. Advisors reached out to approximately 9,000 new students to help them develop individual academic plans. Throughout the semester, advisors reached out to students with high-risk profiles, publicized activities designed to help students become more engaged in the college, and were accessible to students for follow-up questions or discussions.

The initial results of this effort were promising. Half of the students who attended boot camp placed at least one level higher in developmental education. More than twice as many academic plans were completed than in the prior year (about 70% of the 9,000 new students met with an advisor and completed an academic plan during the fall 2012 launch of the new system). Retention for students who met with an advisor and developed a plan was 8 percentage points higher than retention for other incoming students who did not meet with an advisor.

From an operational standpoint, implementing the new intake system provided the foundation for other reforms because it created the infrastructure through which entering students would create an educational plan and choose a program pathway and community of interest. Launching the redesigned intake process was an important "early win" for MDC that demonstrated that large-scale change is possible and that students would benefit as a result. The success of the endeavor was widely communicated across the college. As one administrator commented, "This has been a dynamic and highly energizing experience. There was substantial skepticism in the beginning that any real change would transpire. ... There is broader belief in the possibility of positive change at this point in the process." This highly visible process of reforming the new student intake infrastructure at the college also motivated faculty to work on creating more structured program pathways and to volunteer to coach and mentor students in their programs.

Strengthening Supports Along the Pathway

Based on the initial positive results from the restructured intake process and the added revenue generated as a result of improved retention, the college's senior leadership approved the addition of 25 new full-time positions for advisors (with master's degrees) to expand and enhance the support services offered to new students and to free up the existing advisors to better support returning students. This required an investment of $1 million, for which the college used its own operating funds, as opposed to grant funds, since the new advisors would be an ongoing annual expense. Consistent with the new model of advising that supports students from admission to graduation, the college also transitioned approximately 3,200 students from the 2012–2013 cohorts to academic coaches and mentors to provide more targeted career, transfer, and employment guidance in students' particular program areas. More than 150 faculty, department chairs, and departmental advisors volunteered to coach and mentor students from the time they complete 25% of their program requirements until they graduate. Each academic coach and mentor is supported by a peer in student services.

The college also implemented another key component of the new advising system: precollege advising, which begins in high school and continues until the mandatory orientation, when newly matriculated students are assigned an advisor. While the new system is designed to serve all incoming students, including nontraditional students who have been out of school for some time, the college chose to focus early implementation on incoming high school students because advisors are able to work with them, starting in high school, to set a new paradigm for wraparound advisement support that follows the student throughout his or her career at the college.

Starting in spring 2013, the college began providing additional outreach to high school students, both at the high schools during the spring semester and over the summer prior to enrollment, with the objective of building enthusiasm for attending MDC and increasing early student engagement with the college. College administrators believe that this helped to increase the rate at which recent high school graduates enrolled directly at MDC in the 2013 fall term by 13% over the prior year.

The student services staff and faculty who support students at each stage of the redesigned advising model received extensive training, including classroom instruction and hands-on practice. For example, the advising staff trained the student coaches on how to access and use individual academic plans, how to communicate effectively with students, and how to incorporate advising "best practices" developed by the National Academic Advising Association into their work. Faculty were required to do four hours of "job shadowing" with a professional advisor. In addition, a college-wide learning day was held in March 2013 with a focus on supporting students in and out of the classroom, teaching and learning, and engaging students in the classroom and beyond. Learning was hands on, and participants were exposed to strategies and tools they could integrate into their daily interactions with students and colleagues.

Ensuring Version 2.0 Is Better Than Version 1.0

MDC expects that redesigning its programs and services as described here will enable students to make faster progress and complete their programs of study at a higher rate—and with fewer excess credits—than did similar students in past years. The college is carefully monitoring several near-to-mid-term measures, including course pass rates, retention rates, student satisfaction, and particularly the time it takes students to complete 25% of their program requirements—this may signal that longer term improvements are forthcoming. The college is also systematically evaluating its work on each major aspect of the reforms. The rationale for this is simple: The college cannot create an improved version "2.0" or "3.0" if stakeholders do not understand what worked, what did not work, and how to make it better. An internal evaluation team, led by the college's director of institutional research and planning, has "embedded" research staff members in the redesign implementation teams. These researchers are responsible for documenting the work in each area for use in formative evaluation against logic maps created for each implementation activity. In spring 2013, the college provided training to members of the implementation teams and the internal evaluators on developing and executing a robust evaluation plan.

This evaluation methodology is intended to stimulate ongoing learning and improvement. Evaluation of MDC's initial experience with the redesigned intake system in the summer and fall of 2012 resulted in extensive ideas for improvement that were implemented in the summer of 2013. The college also evaluated the process by which the pathways were mapped, surveying faculty who were involved for their feedback. UPP members recommended the creation of a "tool kit" and training in curriculum development and active learning for teams that will map out pathways in other program areas.

Conclusion: Keys to Making Big Changes

Reflecting on what has enabled MDC to make such changes in a short period, we believe that it was critical that the college's president, Dr. Eduardo Padrón, set the vision for the initiative—and pledged to provide dedicated resources to support it, including full-time staff to coordinate planning and implementation. At the same time, Dr. Padrón let the design, planning, and implementation processes happen from the bottom up. Big changes would likely not have occurred had he dictated solutions to be implemented. The reforms also benefited from a planning year, when faculty, staff, and administrators throughout the college could spend time deliberating about what changes were needed to improve student outcomes.

Continuous, consistent communication has also been essential to the initiative's success and sustainability. Early on, there was a lot of confusion about goals and expectations—as well as a healthy amount of skepticism. Clear communication with faculty, staff, and administrators about ongoing reforms was necessary to overcome that skepticism. Organizing communications across an institution of MDC's size has been challenging. Each reform planning team is responsible for communicating findings they deem important and has spent considerable time deliberating how best to do this. To support the teams and to organize formal messaging, the college appointed a full-time communications person for the initiative. Timely communication to the campuses about research findings and lessons learned has facilitated problem solving and decision making, increased innovation and risk taking, and improved execution.

Transparent and open communication was also essential in working with the faculty union. The discussion about creating more prescribed pathways raised concerns that particular courses could be discontinued, especially among developmental education instructors, whose courses had seen declining enrollments in recent years as the result of improvements at the K–12 level. Frequent communication and the direct involvement of key union leaders in many of the planning and implementation teams paved the way for a successful collaboration with the faculty union.

The biggest threat to the big changes MDC has implemented in a short time was organizational inertia—the mindset that things should be done a certain way because "this is how we have always done things." Communicating frequently about progress, building consensus, and creating a sense of urgency were essential to creating shared ownership and generating progress and momentum. The number of champions for this work has increased dramatically. Today, more than half of all faculty, staff, and administrators are directly involved in one or more implementation activities, and the change they are driving is becoming ingrained in the culture of the institution.

Reference

Padrón, E. J. (2009, May 29). How assessment works at one community college. *The Chronicle of Higher Education.* Retrieved from http://chronicle.com/article/How-Assessment-Works-at-One/44257/

LENORE RODICIO is the provost of Academic and Student Affairs for Miami Dade College.

SUSAN MAYER is a senior partner for completion at Miami Dade College and a leadership coach for Achieving the Dream. She has been embedded full time at Miami Dade College since September 2011.

DAVIS JENKINS is a senior research associate at the Community College Research Center at Columbia University's Teachers College.

NEW DIRECTIONS FOR COMMUNITY COLLEGES • DOI: 10.1002/cc

7

This chapter describes the concurrent reforms occurring in North Carolina—both campus-level changes focused on such issues as developing structured programs of study and state-level reforms aimed at supporting the campus efforts.

State-Level Reforms That Support College-Level Program Changes in North Carolina

R. Edward Bowling, Sharon Morrissey, George M. Fouts

In the spring of 2011, a cadre of five North Carolina community colleges, led by Guilford Technical Community College (GTCC), was awarded a Completion by Design (CBD) grant from the Bill & Melinda Gates Foundation (BMGF). The initiative, announced during President Obama's White House Summit on Community Colleges the previous fall, proposes that intentional, systematic, and structural changes are necessary for colleges to significantly improve graduation rates. CBD also builds upon several key principles: that community colleges' historical emphasis on open access will be maintained, that program quality will not be reduced, and that overall costs will not increase significantly.

This chapter discusses North Carolina's reforms conducted through CBD, focusing on scaling efforts. Now, almost three years later, the five North Carolina community colleges involved in CBD have dramatically altered most students' pathways from initial contact through completion. At the same time, significant local and state policy changes support this work and provide a promising foundation for scaling the work of CBD across all 58 community colleges in the state.

The North Carolina Community College System

Knowing something about the North Carolina Community College System and particularly about its governance is essential to understanding how the North Carolina CBD cadre has been able to quickly gain traction in scaling the CBD initiative far beyond the five cadre colleges. The system celebrated

NEW DIRECTIONS FOR COMMUNITY COLLEGES, no. 167, Fall 2014 © 2014 Wiley Periodicals, Inc.
Published online in Wiley Online Library (wileyonlinelibrary.com) • DOI: 10.1002/cc.20112

its 50th anniversary in 2013. During the first decades of the system's history, community colleges operated under the State Board of Public Instruction, but, in 1981, the legislature established a State Board of Community Colleges to govern the system. The board is empowered by general statutes with considerable rule-making authority to establish policies, practices, and standards for the entire system. The state board selects the system president and it must approve all new college presidents.

Because of the rule-making authority of the state board, the system president has considerable opportunity and responsibility to drive state policy for community colleges in North Carolina. As a result, there is an inevitable tension between the system office and the state board, and the local colleges and their respective boards of trustees. Previous system presidents and Dr. Scott Ralls, the current president of the system, established a de facto arrangement through which the system president fully involves the North Carolina Association of Community College Presidents and often the North Carolina Association of Community College Trustees in the creation and vetting of policy actions that are ultimately going to be considered by the state board.

In 2008, when Dr. Ralls was selected as the 7th president of the system, he and his senior staff began a system-wide listening tour focused on learning about best practices for, as well as obstacles to, fostering student success. Based on those findings and working with the presidents' association and the trustees' association, the state board in 2010 launched SuccessNC, a three-year strategic initiative to dramatically improve student outcomes across the system through developmental education redesign, structured dual enrollment programs, transitions programs for basic skills students, stackable credentials in technical programs, financial aid simplification, and analytic data tools. It is that foundation that informs the work of Completion by Design in North Carolina. In addition, the North Carolina Community College System Office (NCCCSO) serves as state policy lead for the cadre and is tasked with (a) developing a policy framework to support the cadre's work and (b) working with GTCC to develop and implement a scaling strategy for North Carolina.

CBD Planning Year 2011–2012

GTCC was selected as the "managing partner," or lead college, for the cadre because of its past success with Achieving the Dream (ATD) and with a Developmental Education Initiative (DEI) grant. GTCC was one of the inaugural ATD colleges selected for a Lumina Foundation grant in 2004. Through that grant, GTCC focused on increasing student success by using data to improve programs and services for students. Later, in 2009, GTCC was selected as one of 15 community colleges nationwide to participate in the DEI, an initiative that enabled colleges to expand innovative developmental education work begun or evolved from their ATD efforts. In 2010, GTCC received the Leah Meyer Austin Award as the outstanding ATD college.

Other community colleges participating in the North Carolina CBD cadre are Davidson County Community College (DCCC), Central Piedmont Community College (CPCC), Wake Technical Community College (WTCC), and Martin Community College (MCC). Each of the colleges has a record of developing initiatives to improve student success. All but one are members of the ATD network. In addition, the cadre was designed to represent the diversity of the 58 community colleges that make up the North Carolina system. GTCC, WTCC, and CPCC are large, urban, multicampus institutions; DCCC is a midsized college serving a suburban area; and MCC is a small, rural college in eastern North Carolina. A primary reason for the planning group wanting to have this sort of diversity in the cadre was its desire to ultimately scale the CBD work across the system. Therefore, it was thought important to learn how such an initiative worked in both small and large colleges.

Through the first six months of the planning year, each college assembled a core working team under the direction of a project lead. The composition of the teams varied by college; some relied more heavily on administrators, while others mixed faculty and midlevel staff together. In every case, the team represented the broad array of instructional and student service support roles. Likewise, the project leads varied among faculty and administrators. The teams analyzed seven years of student data seeking to diagnose students' major loss points and momentum points along their academic pathways. This analysis was based on the prior work of the BMGF that produced a loss/momentum framework (see Figure 7.1) that segments students' progress into four phases: connection (interest to application), entry (enrollment to completion of gatekeeper courses), progress (entry into course of study to 75% of requirements completed), and completion (complete course of study and transition/transfer). The analyses showed that there were both common and unique loss and momentum points across the colleges.

During this period, the cadre held quarterly retreats, allowing the teams to gather and discuss findings and recommendations for improving completion rates. At each of these retreats, leadership was provided by the cadre's executive director, a GTCC employee, who was responsible for coordinating the work across the colleges, and the senior partner, who worked closely with the senior administrators at the colleges to build institutional support. The cadre also benefitted from the guidance of a variety of national assistance partners including the Community College Research Center, Jobs for the Future, Public Agenda, the RP Group, WestEd, and the CBD Assistance Team, a group assembled to launch the initiative and coordinate the planning year across the state cadres.

In addition to college personnel, system office staff also participated in these retreats. Frequently during the retreat discussions, participants cited

Figure 7.1.   Loss and Momentum Framework

Loss/Momentum Framework			
Connection	Entry	Progress	Completion
Interest to Application	Enrollment to Completion of Gatekeeper Courses	Entry into Course of Study to 75% Requirements Completed	Complete Course of Study to Credential with Labor Market Value
Institutional Focus on Completion			
Effective Use of Technology to Support Engagement			
Policies That Promote Student Success			

what they thought were system policies that prevented innovation. Often, the system staff pointed out that such a system policy did not exist or that it had been misinterpreted. Sometimes, it turned out to be a local policy that was a barrier. The system office staff also listened for possible system policy implications that arose during the cadre's planning.

As the college teams conducted their data analysis, they began to share their results with the faculty and staff at their colleges. Preliminary conclusions were also tested through focus groups, including focus groups with students. Based on the quantitative analysis and on input provided through the focus groups, as well as additional data collected via surveys, the teams identified several factors associated with student exit between connection and completion: the high percentage of entering students needing developmental education, the failure of the college to provide adequate and consistent academic advisement and career exploration, financial barriers, and academic programs that needed more structure.

While four of the five North Carolina colleges had completed extensive data analysis as a component of their work for ATD, CBD forced the teams to examine a much larger seven-year set of data on all of their students. Usually, ATD initiatives focus on a more specific group of students and/or a specific segment of the students' journey at the college. CBD required analyzing students' entire journey, which then led to rethinking all aspects of the college—administrative, instructional, and student services—and how they need to work together. CBD seeks major, not incremental, improvements in student success.

Approximately five months into the planning year, the local teams and the cadre as a whole shifted the focus to the design of a clearer, prescriptive student pathway through college that would be intentionally planned to improve overall completion rates. As with the data analysis phase, support was available from the CBD national assistance team. For example, they collaborated to develop a set of design principles that guided the cadre's work. In addition, the colleges did their own extensive review of successful and promising practices developed through ATD and the DEI. As this new completion pathway was being designed, there were multiple opportunities for the CBD teams to vet their work with the national partners, with the CBD cadres in other states, and on their own campuses.

As the planning year drew to a close, the North Carolina CBD team settled on the five major strategies it would propose to the BMGF for funding support:

- Create more prescriptive programs of study aligned with the demands of the local job markets or the requirements for junior standing for a baccalaureate degree.
- Reduce the number of students referred to developmental education and accelerate the movement of referred students into well-defined and prescriptive programs of study.
- Redesign student service practices and processes to provide better student advisement, early alert, and referrals to interventions and instructional supports.
- Implement new technologies to support academic planning and student services.
- Develop a comprehensive plan to obtain temporary policy waivers and longer term local and statewide policy changes that support student completion.

Relying on both proven and promising practices and the identification of common momentum and loss points among the five colleges, the cadre's pathway design began with the end in mind. That is, any student pathway must lead either to meaningful employment or to successful transfer. The student experience contains a variety of new practices to mitigate issues that cause students to drop out and to strengthen major events where students seem to gain momentum in their progress toward completion. Creation of this new pathway required significant policy changes at both the local and system levels.

Changes in Policy and Practice

Shortly after the announcement of North Carolina's award of a planning grant, Dr. Ralls, in conjunction with the cadre college presidents, named a State Advisory Board for the initiative. This board includes the cadre college presidents, other North Carolina community college presidents, State Board of Community College members, local trustees, the state superintendent for public schools, a representative from the General Administration of the University of North Carolina, and some key business leaders in North Carolina. The advisory board held its first meeting on the day of the state's CBD kickoff.

As the planning year closed, the NCCCSO staff members who had been participating in the cadre retreats developed a comprehensive list of policy implications raised by the cadre's work and the proposed new pathway to completion. A total of nine state-level policy changes were recommended, and six additional local policy areas were recommended for review by each cadre college. The policy levers fell into four categories: those that would require legislative action, those that would involve cooperative effort with the K–12 system or the university system, those that would need to be addressed by the State Board of Community Colleges, and those that could be addressed at the local college level. The policies are listed in Table 7.1.

Working with the CBD State Advisory Board and the Core State Policy Team (the CBD presidents, NCCCSO president and chief academic officer, and the cadre leadership), a plan was developed to address each of the policy issues during the two-year implementation period. The Advisory Board and the Policy Team identified three of those policy priorities as having the greatest potential to impact students' success and colleges' completion rates during the first three years and the greatest potential for supporting scale-up of the CBD completion pathways:

- Allow alternative methods for placing students; allow students who place near college-ready to enroll concurrently in developmental education and college-level courses: Revise the State Board of Community Colleges' student placement and developmental education prerequisite policies to (a) allow research-validated, alternative methods for determining a student's college readiness instead of relying on a single test score and (b) allow colleges to enroll students who place near college-ready in college courses with corequisite developmental or supplemental instruction, instead of requiring the developmental instruction as a prerequisite.
- Create highly structured programs: Revise the NCCCS curriculum standards to facilitate highly structured programs of study at the college level by: (a) using the Department of Education CIP codes, clustering similar programs with a standard template; (b) creating a common technical core track for programs within the same cluster; and (c)

Table 7.1 Policy Levers Used to Scale North Carolina's Efforts

Policy Levers	Status
Legislative Policy Levers (1) Provide Summer Funding (Budget FTE) to Accelerate Student Success (*Entry*) (2) Provide Incentives for Persistence and Completion (*Completion*)	• S.L. 2013 provided summer funding for dev. ed. and STEM programs. • Performance-based funding implemented 2013; included student progress and completion measures. • Legislature asked for study to increase transfer enrollment in NCCCS.
K–12 and Higher Education Alignment Policy Levers (3) Align K–12 Common Core Standards and Assessments With College-Ready Standards (*Connection*) (4) Update the Comprehensive Articulation Agreement (*Progress, Completion*) • Ensure that all CAA general education core courses transfer for course credit. • Ensure that students who complete the AA/AS enter the university with junior standing. • Develop policies and procedures to support reverse transfer of credit.	• Received *Core to College* grant for 2012–2015 to support alignment. • K–12 State Board of Education implemented *Career Ready* and *College Ready* diploma endorsements. • CAA Revision in process: 30 Hour General Education Component guaranteed to transfer for course equivalency credit; AA/AS completers guaranteed to enter university with junior standing. • *Credit When It's Due* reverse transfer pilot underway.
State Board of Community Colleges Policy Levers (5) Allow Alternative Methods for Placing Students (*Entry*) • Allow use of high school transcript GPA for placement instead of relying on a single assessment. • Allow students who place near college-ready to enroll concurrently in developmental education and college-level course.	• SBCC implemented Multiple Measure Policy to allow high school GPA as a placement measure; also allows concurrent enrollment in developmental and college-level courses for students who place near college ready in reading, English, and math.

(Continued)

Table 7.1 Continued

Policy Levers	Status
(6) Create Highly Structured Programs (*Progress*)	
• Restructure curriculum standards to enable colleges to clearly map out program requirements and course sequencing.	• Curriculum standards for programs reviewed in *Code Green Super CIP* revised to develop structured programs of study with stackable credentials.
• Provide opportunities for "stackable" credentials with multiple entry and exit points.	
(7) Revise College Foundation of NC Common Application (*Connection*)	• *In Progress*
• Allow "Undecided, Degree-Seeking" option so that students don't pick an unintended major at the application stage that potentially sets them on the wrong course.	
(8) Implement Degree Mapping Technology (*Progress*)	• *In Progress at Completion by Design Colleges*
(9) Develop/Implement Guidelines to Award Credit for Prior Learning/Credit for CE Credential (*Progress*)	• *In Progress*
College Policy Levers	
(10) Require a Student Success Course for Students in Developmental Education (*Entry*)	
(11) Require Orientation (*Entry*)	
(12) Develop Mandatory Placement Test Preparation Course (*Entry*)	
(13) Develop Early Alert Systems (*Progress*)	
(14) Revise program structures to Reduce Elective Options (*Progress*)	
(15) Establish No Late Registration Policy (*Entry, Progress*)	

providing opportunities for stackable credentials with multiple entry and exit points. Structured programs of study that share a common technical core provide opportunities for students to complete credentials for entry-level employment and return to college later to add on additional credentials or complete an associate's degree.

- Update the Comprehensive Articulation Agreement: Revise the Comprehensive Articulation Agreement between the NCCCS and the University of North Carolina's 16 constituent institutions to develop structured pathways to majors and reduce elective options by: (a) identifying the most popular transfer majors and developing structured pathways that better track students into major pathways, (b) ensuring that all general education core courses transfer for course credit, (c) ensuring that students who complete the AA/AS degrees enter the university on track to complete the BA/BS in two years, and (d) creating statewide policies and procedures to allow students who transfer early to transfer credit back to the community college to fulfill requirements for the associate degree.

All of the groups who reviewed the list of policy implications developed during the cadre's planning year agreed that these three policy priorities strongly supported the cadre's focus on more prescriptive programs of study, reduction in the numbers of students referred to developmental education and acceleration of those referred students through developmental education into their programs of study, and a redesign of academic advising that places more emphasis on academic planning and student/advisor engagement. Since the adoption of this policy agenda, considerable progress has been made on the three key levers.

Allow Alternative Placement Approaches.   The State Board of Community Colleges has the authority to establish testing and placement policies for students entering any of the 58 community colleges. The long-standing policy established statewide cutoff scores for English, reading, and mathematics and required all new students to take a placement test to determine their enrollment in developmental or credit level courses. Additionally, board policy required that developmental prerequisites be completed before enrolling in credit level coursework.

The data analysis performed using the loss/momentum framework showed clearly that the major loss point for students was developmental education. Sixty-five percent of students in the North Carolina cadre colleges begin their programs in at least one developmental course, and research shows that such students are unlikely to complete a credential (Bailey, 2009). Therefore, the North Carolina CBD completion pathway includes a variety of interventions to either eliminate or accelerate developmental education for some students.

Fortunately, the North Carolina DEI State Policy Council, which was formed in 2009, had already done considerable work in the redesign of developmental education across the 58 colleges that make up the North Carolina system. By the time CBD began, a developmental math faculty team from colleges across the system had begun to develop a modularized form of developmental math, and all five CBD colleges were already offering that format. In addition, the redesign of developmental English and reading into a combined, modularized format is also moving toward system-wide implementation. This effort in North Carolina has been directly modeled after the developmental redesign done in Virginia (Asera, 2011).

The modularized format allows students to move more quickly through developmental education and to complete only the content necessary for success in their chosen program of study. In 2012, the state board approved awarding a contract for the development of a diagnostic placement tool that allows better matching of students' needs to developmental modules. The contractor, College Board, has completed the developmental math portion and will release the developmental reading/English in spring 2014. Achieving this change required not only the work of the DEI State Policy Council but also of the NCCCSO, which vetted a proposal through the North Carolina Association of Community College Presidents and ultimately to the State Board of Community Colleges in order to make state-level policy changes.

The NCCCSO also contracted with the Community College Research Center (CCRC) to conduct a multiple measures study to determine if some measure other than placement tests was a valid predictor of student success. The results of that CCRC study were first presented to the DEI State Policy Council, which developed a proposal for using high school grade point average (GPA) as an alternative measure for placement. That proposal went through extensive vetting by the presidents' association, instructional and student services administrators' organizations, and finally by the state board, which approved the new policy in February of 2013.

Create Highly Structured Programs.   The effort to realign programs of study was largely based on the research by Jenkins and Cho (2012) demonstrating that students who concentrate in a defined program of study during their first year of enrollment are far more likely to eventually graduate than those who select a variety of electives from a smorgasbord of course offerings. Each cadre college worked with a broad range of faculty to redesign their traditional transfer degrees and selected technical degrees. This work was difficult because it challenged assumptions long held and strongly endorsed, especially by arts and science faculty. Focus groups conducted by individual colleges during the planning year and supplemented by some independent focus groups conducted by Public Agenda confirmed that students, particularly those who dropped out, believed that a more regimented program of study would have been helpful to their progress.

Update the Comprehensive Articulation Agreement.   The concepts driving structured programs of study informed the recent revision of North Carolina's Comprehensive Articulation Agreement (CAA). The CAA, which has been in place since 1997, guarantees completion of undergraduate general education requirements if the student completes a 44-hour core or an associate's degree prior to transfer. However, a recent analysis of transfer student data revealed that only 13% of NCCCS transfer students completed the general education core prior to transferring, thus negating the transfer guarantees established in the CAA. Many students found that their courses transferred as elective credits rather than course credits, thus increasing their cost and time to completion after transfer. Part of the problem is the number of elective options in colleges' programs of study, and part of the problem is that North Carolina's public universities do not have common course numbering or common general education requirements. Typically, transfer students are offered extensive "pick lists" of general education courses, and they select courses without understanding that some of those courses will transfer as elective credit rather than course credit if they transfer before completing the AA or AS degree.

The proposed solution is to (a) create a highly structured program of study for college transfer students and (b) provide better advising to encourage students to complete the AA or AS degree prior to transferring. The new AA and AS degree programs will include a 30-hour universal general education transfer block of courses guaranteed to transfer to any of the state's 16 public universities for course equivalency credit. Within this block, students will have limited elective options. But they will enroll in a College Transfer Success Course during which they will select a transfer major and university and map out their remaining 30 hours of general education and premajor courses, depending on the chosen major pathway and transfer university. For students who transfer early, each of the courses identified in the universal general education transfer block will transfer for course credit to any of the 16 universities. Students who complete the AA or AS degree prior to transfer will receive 60 hours of transfer credit and move into the major as juniors. The new college transfer program will be implemented in the fall semester of 2014.

Preparing for Scale

In order the lay the groundwork for a large scaling effort, leaders in North Carolina worked to get traction with stakeholders who had not originally been involved, made plans to include additional colleges, and developed a student success learning institute. Those efforts are described briefly below.

Gaining Traction With Other Stakeholders.   As stated in the introduction, intentional thought was given early to how the initiative could eventually be scaled across the system. During the planning year, efforts were made to inform the entire system about the work of the cadre. That work started with the CBD State Advisory Board. This group was well-positioned to respond to the pathway plan as it developed, and also to be an advocacy group for the policy changes that would inevitably follow.

Just as CBD campus teams kept their own college communities aware of the planning activities, the North Carolina cadre leadership reached out to system organizations such as the presidents, the chief academic officers, and the chief student service officers. During the planning year, the NCCCSO also redesigned its SuccessNC website around the CBD loss/momentum framework and organized the many student success initiatives around the connection, entry, progress, and completion framework.

At quarterly meetings, the CBD presidents and Dr. Ralls received regular updates on progress. Dr. Randy Parker, president of GTCC, and Dr. Ralls opened those quarterly briefings to other presidents within the system, and by spring of 2012, 21 of those presidents attended. In addition, experts from the partner organizations as well as the cadre and project leads made presentations to the presidents' association about CBD issues. And, at another quarterly meeting of the association, the cadre leadership and the project leads from each of the five colleges made a major presentation on the completion pathway.

In 2012, the presidents' association launched a two-year professional development program to bring national speakers to their meetings to share emerging research and promising practices related to all aspects of the CBD work. In addition to the college president, a senior administrator from each college is participating in these sessions. Also, the trustees' association has created a program with its members entitled "Trustee Engagement in Student Success & Completion Initiatives in North Carolina."

Finally, the cadre prepared for scaling by frequently analyzing college-level data and meeting to discuss the implications of findings. For example, the CBD cadre assesses their progress through a set of key performance indicators (KPIs) developed for the CBD states in cooperation with some of the national assistance partners. The KPIs include short-term measures, such as semester-to-semester persistence and the percentage of students who accumulate six or more curriculum credit hours in their first semester, as well as longer term measures like program completion rates. Additional qualitative research is being conducted by MDRC.

CBD 2.0.   Near the end of the 2011–2012 planning year, a request was made to the BMGF to use some remaining funds to involve four additional North Carolina community colleges in the CBD work. These colleges (Durham Technical CC, Stanly CC, Gaston College, and Asheville-Buncombe Technical CC) were chosen because of their involvement in ATD, their demonstrated commitment to evidence-based student success reforms, and the interest their presidents had expressed during the quarterly CBD briefings described above. We anticipate they will be ready to begin implementation of their new pathways during fall of 2014.

North Carolina Student Success Learning Institute.   As the first implementation year finished in July 2013, the NCCCSO partnered with GTCC to plan the North Carolina Student Success Learning Institute (SSLI). Building on the scaling work begun with CBD 2.0, SSLI provided senior leadership teams from 27 community colleges an opportunity to be immersed in the framework and activities of CBD. An intensive, two-day convening launched SSLI in October 2013. There, college teams comprised of the chief academic and student service officers, institutional research heads, and a faculty member learned about the major components of the North Carolina structured pathways. The event was led by the CBD national assistance team and leadership from the CBD cadre colleges.

During the next six months, a series of webinars and web-based assignments guided each of the SSLI colleges to develop an action plan to incorporate the Completion by Design framework and strategies. The colleges reconvened in May 2014 to share their action plans and receive feedback from other colleges and national experts. The plans were then finalized and delivered to each college's president for implementation. A second SSLI will be launched in fall 2014 for the remaining North Carolina colleges.

Conclusion

As the work of implementation continues at the original CBD colleges, and the work begins at other North Carolina community colleges, the cadre leadership has spent an extensive amount of time considering the lessons that have been learned over the past two and a half years. Those initial lessons, summarized below, will be shared broadly:

- Colleges desiring to pursue CBD must be deeply committed to the use of data, combined with developing a meaningful of a culture of inquiry into that data, in order to improve student success. Certainly, experience with a program such as ATD is desirable.
- While ATD initiatives are usually focused on analyzing and improving a particular segment of the student pathway, CBD seeks to improve the total pathway. Therefore, engagement of the total college community is necessary for success in this venture.
- Eliminating or accelerating developmental education is essential if completion rates are to improve dramatically.
- Early connection of students, including students needing developmental education, to the activities and resources of the college appears to be a key component of ensuring their later success.
- Making programs of study more restrictive by reducing the number of elective options will hopefully increase student completion.
- Effective student service support along the entire pathway, from connection to completion, is equally important. Engagement of faculty, staff, and students throughout the redesign process is both helpful to the planning process and absolutely essential for implementation of the resulting changes.

Since CBD is such a comprehensive redesign effort, the greatest lesson learned to date is the tremendous depth of cultural change required to successfully implement such an integrated web of structural and policy changes. That sort of cultural change ultimately depends on committed leadership from presidents (and their boards of trustees), faculty, and staff. In the case of North Carolina, where the intent to scale was intentional from the beginning, that commitment also includes the system leadership.

References

Asera, R. (2011). *Innovation at scale: How Virginia community colleges are collaborating to improve developmental education and increase student success.* Boston, MA: Jobs for the Future.

Bailey, T. (2009, February). *Rethinking developmental education in community college* (Brief No. 40). New York, NY: Community College Research Center, Teachers College, Columbia University.

Jenkins, D., & Cho, S.-W. (2012, January). *Get with the program: Accelerating community college students' entry into and completion of programs of study.* New York, NY: Community College Research Center, Teachers College, Columbia University.

R. EDWARD BOWLING *is the executive director of North Carolina's Completion by Design initiative.*

SHARON MORRISSEY *was the executive vice president and chief academic officer for the North Carolina Community College System at the time of writing this chapter. She is now the vice chancellor for Academic Services and Research for the Virginia Community College System.*

GEORGE M. FOUTS *is the senior partner for North Carolina's Completion by Design Initiative.*

NEW DIRECTIONS FOR COMMUNITY COLLEGES • DOI: 10.1002/cc

8

*This chapter focuses on how colleges can increase faculty,
administrator, and staff engagement in reform processes, with the
message that large-scale change is not merely technical work; there
is a powerful human dimension that can make or break a reform.*

What We've Learned About Supporting
Faculty, Administrator, and Staff
Engagement

Alison Kadlec, Isaac Rowlett

Community colleges today are navigating turbulent times, squeezed from
within and outside by shrinking resources, growing competition, and increasingly complex student populations with diverse needs. Between national initiatives and campus-level reform efforts aimed at helping more
students achieve their goals, most colleges are also awash in student success pilots, projects, and programs. While some of these efforts are having
significant positive impacts on student outcomes in small pockets, far too
many good ideas and promising innovations intend to scale, but are not
successful. Some ideas fail to gain traction because they're too costly, im-
practical, or inherently flawed, but evidence from a range of fields suggests
that most failures of innovation are in fact failures of implementation (Heath
& Heath, 2010; Klein & Knight, 2005; Rogers, 2003).

Understanding why great ideas fail to take hold as institutionalized solutions is a critical piece of the community college student success puzzle. The diversity of community college contexts adds complexity to the
analysis; community colleges cannot be painted with a single brush in this
enterprise. Size, access to resources, geographical circumstance, policy environment, and governance structure have powerful and distinct impacts
on how student success efforts are designed and implemented.

At the same time, there are critical cross-cutting lessons that speak to
shared features of all community colleges, public higher education change
efforts in general, and perhaps all public sector innovation efforts. The
features that often hinder community college change efforts are related
to their multimission nature and the fact that a majority, sometimes an

New Directions for Community Colleges, no. 167, Fall 2014 © 2014 Wiley Periodicals, Inc.
Published online in Wiley Online Library (wileyonlinelibrary.com) • DOI: 10.1002/cc.20113

overwhelming majority, of courses are taught by adjunct faculty who face special challenges and generally lack the security and privileges that come with long-term job stability (Kezar & Sam, 2010).

More generally, the lessons of institutional reform speak to concerns related to the human side of change, in which institutional culture and climate are the primary vehicles for sense-making. In this realm, the focus is on the interplay between an institution's history, undergirding values, dominant dispositions, mission, and conditions in which its faculty, staff, and administrators operate (Ewell, 2008; Shugart, 2012). The points of intervention here typically relate to habits, patterns, and structures of communication and inquiry at various levels within and across institution or system. While there is a firm and growing research base on these issues in relatively new fields like implementation science and mature fields like organizational psychology, higher education lags in both research and especially practice (Brownson, Colditz, & Proctor, 2012; Henderson, Dancy, & Niewiadomska-Bugaj, 2012; Jex & Britt, 2008; Kezar & Sam, 2010; Klein & Knight, 2005).

We take this opportunity to share key lessons that the authors and the rest of our team at Public Agenda have learned from on-the-ground stakeholder engagement work with dozens of community college systems, more than a hundred individual colleges and thousands of institutional practitioners from across the country. Driven by a mission to help diverse leaders and publics make progress on complex and divisive issues, our practical work focuses on strengthening the capacity of institutional leaders at every level to create high-functioning and healthy communities. By "healthy" and "high-functioning," we mean those that are anchored by a deep, shared commitment to improved outcomes for students and in which creative collaboration, an improvement mindset, and mutual respect across professional boundaries are norms. In our work with community colleges we play many different roles including researcher, thought-partner, convening designer, facilitator, mediator, troubleshooter, and occasional provocateur. In our roles we bring knowledge and expertise from fields like social psychology, change management, implementation science, and deliberative democracy to the work of fostering improved collaboration among and between institutional practitioners on behalf of shared student success goals. At its best, skillful and authentic engagement of faculty, staff, and administrators can significantly improve the quality of decision making, accelerate progress on difficult issues, and create the conditions for good ideas to become sustainable solutions. In the absence of strong engagement practices, not even the best ideas are likely to live long enough to fulfill their potential.

In the next section, we summarize the main lessons we have learned through the design and facilitation of hundreds of faculty, student, staff, and administrator focus groups and dozens of internal stakeholder dialogues at colleges of all sizes and types across the country. We focus here primarily on our work to develop cultures of inquiry and collaboration, but we also make an effort to cite relevant literature and empirical research to amplify, contextualize, or sharpen points. We are especially interested in research bases *outside* of higher education in fields like health care, because our experience has shown there is much to learn through interdisciplinary inquiry that seeks to bridge research and practice in new ways.

Finally, we offer a set of practical "checklists" aimed at helping colleges assess both their culture of engagement and the climate around any proposed innovation. The checklists take the form of discussion questions that are best viewed as diagnostic tools that can be used in a variety of ways including during strategic planning processes, in the creation of protocols for focus groups and other kinds of structured listening sessions, and as fodder for survey instruments. For more on how to think about and use checklists, see Atul Gawande's (2009) *Checklist Manifesto*.

Lessons Learned

In this section, we summarize the major lessons learned through Public Agenda's work with community colleges in more than half the states in the United States on issues related to the changing landscape of higher education. In our institutional practitioner engagement efforts, we focus our contributions on framing issues for deliberation, either providing directly or training others to facilitate difficult conversations, and designing convenings and other collaborative working sessions to help faculty, staff, and administrators improve their ability to achieve shared goals.

Across contexts, we have learned that common challenges to sustainable, scalable innovation on behalf of student success include heavy workloads, initiative fatigue, lack of leadership buy-in, resistance to mandates, justifiable fear of change, legitimate arguments against a given initiative, resource constraints, and even disagreement about the nature of the problem. In what follows, we focus on capturing, contextualizing, and illustrating the lessons that we believe are most critical to the work of overcoming these barriers.

Attention to the Human Side of Change.   Many complex problems and the changes they entail are more about values, collective choice, and decision making under conditions of flux and uncertainty, than they are about implementing a clearly defined "fix." In these cases, disagreement about the nature of the problem as well as the proposed value of various solutions is common and greatly complicates any change effort. In his now classic *Leadership Without Easy Answers*, Ronald Heifetz (1994) makes the distinction between technical problems and adaptive problems—technical problems are easy to identify, and lend themselves to cut-and-dried solutions that are expert-driven and successfully implemented by edict. Most of the problems facing community colleges do not fit this description. Instead, most complex challenges are what Heifetz calls "adaptive," meaning they are difficult to unpack (easy to deny) and solving them requires changes in values, beliefs, roles, relationships, and approaches to work. More traditional approaches to understanding and creating institutional change, those that focus narrowly on systems and processes, fail to attend sufficiently to the microlevel practices where systemic and sustainable improvement actually occurs. Those interested in creating lasting change would be well served by remembering H. L. Mencken's famous line: "For every complex problem, there is an answer that is clear, simple, and wrong."

For adaptive problems, people at every level of the organization must play a role in framing issues and in identifying and implementing solutions. Solutions to adaptive challenges generally require change in numerous places across traditional boundaries. Complex problems like those related to community college student success exceed the ability of any one type of expert to understand, much less address or solve. Institutional readiness for change can be gauged and tweaked through ongoing awareness of the changing relationships and shifting attitudes and interpretations of the faculty, staff, and lower-level administrators implicated in a change process. The research base on this is strong and diverse, from the sociological and organizational studies of the "decoupling" of formally adopted changes in policy from the actual practices in the workplace (Edelman, Leachman, & McAdam, 2010; Kellogg, 2012; Meyer & Rowan, 1977), to the current work of change management practitioners and researchers Chip Heath and Dan Heath (2010), and to the now robust field of implementation science. Overall, it is our experience that most people tend to underestimate their ability to influence the human pieces of the change puzzle, and instead look for technical fixes.

Attending to the human side of change entails taking the time to develop and refine processes to bring a wider range of perspectives and insights to the table. This can feel counterintuitive or distracting to leaders, until they see the benefits or experience the costs of failing to do so. We often hear leaders say that they don't have the time to do deep listening with faculty and staff, or that they are afraid of opening a can of worms by attempting to do so. In our experience, however, the time it takes to "do it right" is far less than the time it takes to get back on track once efforts go off the rails because of backlash and resistance from those whose active support is necessary for successful implementation. Doing it right requires early, ongoing, and intentional efforts to seek input and insight from stakeholders. It also entails meaningful follow-up. The payoff is better solutions and a better shot at lasting change because efforts like these foster the trust and relationships that are vital for effective implementation of promising innovations.

Who, When, and How.   Careful attention to the staging and sequencing of engagement efforts is an integral piece of the human side of change. Not every stakeholder needs to be engaged on every issue, but careful design and implementation should include systematic consideration of which stakeholders are critical to engage at which stage. When it comes to faculty engagement, special efforts should be made to reach beyond formal faculty leaders to engage informal leaders, peer influencers, and adjunct faculty who teach a majority of college courses in this country. Finding multiple avenues and higher and lower touch opportunities for engaging busy faculty and staff is helpful and appreciated.

Because the search for solutions depends on improved channels of communication and collaboration, a successful engagement strategy will include an ongoing combination of communications and dialogue. It is essential for leaders to regularly and repeatedly provide clear, accurate, and consistent information about how various student success efforts fit together and how the input of faculty and staff are being used to advance these efforts. Press release–like announcements (either through email or at standing meetings) at critical decision or action points help faculty stay informed and provide them with opportunities to weigh in. Providing multiple opportunities is critical, however, because most institutional practitioners suffer a deluge of emails and it is very easy to lose track of even important communications. While surveys are limited tools for engagement, as part of a larger process they can complement an in-person approach and gather the perspectives of far-flung faculty and staff. Focus groups give small groups of participants opportunities to learn about and work through issues and give project leaders insights into the values, concerns, opinions, and ideas held by individual stakeholder types. Periodic forums attended by larger groups of both instructional and student support staff are opportunities for relationship development and collaborative learning and problem solving on a broader scale. But they can also turn into unproductive gripe sessions, which is why careful design and facilitation is important. Given how busy and stretched thin most faculty, staff, and administrators are, taking the time to carefully sequence engagement activities and provide a range of opportunities for input can signal respect for people's time.

The most sophisticated colleges we have worked with learned to use a combination of engagement strategies to draw on the experience and ideas of faculty, while surfacing and addressing concerns that can become derailers if left unaddressed. For example, one college began a new student success initiative by issuing a brief questionnaire to every faculty and staff member. College leaders enjoyed an overwhelming response rate and took advantage of the wealth of data to inform their initial approach to institutional transformation. The survey results were used to design individual focus groups with faculty, staff, administrators, and students. The report on the outcomes of the focus groups was distributed across the campus, and the conversation it generated helped college leaders identify volunteers to lead and support the implementation process. Because of these systematic and purposeful engagement efforts, college leadership was able to create diverse work teams of motivated individuals from both student support services and the academic side of the institution to push the work forward. This kind of silo-spanning collaboration provided the college with the momentum it needed to make significant progress, while strengthening its culture of collaboration.

The Devil Is in the Details.   Put simply, it is our experience that institutional leaders throw a lot of obstacles in their own paths through clumsy communication, empty-gesture consultation with faculty and staff, poorly structured meetings, overreliance on top-down decision making, and the tendency to use data to bludgeon rather than engage. Without rigorous attention to process-design details, such as how and when people are invited to participate, how issues are framed, the way data are translated for different audiences, and the fairness and quality of facilitation, even the most seemingly uncontroversial and straightforward efforts can breed resistance and hostility among those whose support is required for success. These details are often the first to be overlooked by busy leaders or those tasked with managing change.

One college learned this lesson the hard way when its provost sent an email to faculty requesting their attendance at an "important student success meeting" the following day at noon. Not sure of what to expect but wary of disobeying the provost, faculty canceled meetings, office hours, and even rescheduled classes in order to attend. When they arrived, they were greeted by senior administrators and outside consultants who were introduced as "student success experts" who had been hired to instruct the faculty on how to improve their course completion rates. The faculty didn't exactly embrace the session, and the lack of adequate seating and absence of refreshments did not improve the situation. What may have simply been an oversight on details for leadership had the impact of conveying a lack of respect to faculty.

While the situation described above is perhaps a more extreme case of failure to attend to important details, other mistakes are far more common. For example, too often senior administrators will take the time to hold structured listening sessions with faculty and staff, but will then fail to follow up afterward to let participants know either how their input was used or why it was not used. People can live with decisions they do not like, but they cannot abide feeling that their time has been wasted. It is not enough to send a single email thanking people for their time, though even this basic courtesy is often overlooked by busy senior administrators. Faculty and staff need to hear in many different ways and venues how and why their input is or is not being used. Failure to attend sufficiently to these seemingly mundane communication issues can exacerbate wariness or fuel resistance.

The Focus Belongs on Conditions, Not Personalities.   Most of us are vulnerable to the "fundamental attribution error," which leads us to account for resistance to change by looking at traits of individuals or groups instead of closely examining the context in which those individuals act. Faculty or staff resistance to innovation is better analyzed as a situation problem instead of a people problem because it is much easier to tweak conditions than it is to change *how people are.* Institutional leaders and senior administrators are most successful when they stop viewing faculty or staff resistance as a matter of fundamental character defects (e.g., laziness, unreflective aversion to change) and instead begin by interrogating the features of the contexts these individuals inhabit. Disciplinary characteristics, professional incentives, practices around workflow, habits of communication, and the organizational culture and climate in which resistant faculty members operate are critical to understanding the nature of resistance to change. There are many reasons why one might run into pushback, but laziness is probably not one of them (Heath & Heath, 2010).

The events at one community college illustrate the importance of building capacity for inclusive and meaningful engagement among and between institutional practitioners like faculty and staff. The leaders at this college had kicked off a large-scale student success initiative with a college-wide event intended to motivate faculty and staff about the new effort. Faculty were asked to facilitate breakout groups as part of the event, but it turned out afterward that the faculty facilitators pushed back against the initiative, citing frustration and resistance from their peers. Instead of dismissing the faculty facilitators' opposition as simply a knee-jerk response, college leaders listened carefully to them. In doing so the leaders discovered that the pushback emerged not out of a desire to maintain the status quo, but instead it came from a lack of confidence and unfamiliarity with the concepts and terminology. The faculty facilitators needed professional development in areas such facilitation and conflict resolution to equip them with the necessary tools to discuss student success with their colleagues.

The college leaders recalibrated their strategy by slowing down the process and provided additional training and support to faculty team members from each department. In doing so, college leaders became partners with faculty, who then became empowered to advance positive changes within their departments. Several members of this core faculty group, some of whom hold leadership positions in the college's vociferous faculty union, presented their work alongside college leaders at a national conference. Both the faculty and administrators described the experience as critical to the college's improved student outcomes in recent years.

Change Leadership Is More Important Than Change Management. For community colleges seeking to innovate around student success and achievement, the distinction between *change management* and *change leadership* is especially useful and instructive. According to change management expert John Kotter, change management is a set of processes, tools, and mechanisms that are best designed to push along small-scale changes in tightly controlled ways. Change leadership on the other hand "concerns the driving forces, visions and processes that fuel large-scale transformation" (Kotter, 2011, para. 1). Change leadership is defined as the driving engine of change, an engine fueled by big vision and by empowering many different people within and across an organization. Unlike discrete change-management efforts that focus on minimizing surprises, change leadership is about accelerating everyone's shared appreciation of the urgency and value of significant change. Change leadership is less about tight control of discrete processes and more about galvanizing shared desire for change and, therefore, it can take unexpected directions that are best viewed as opportunities to be seized rather than distractions to be squelched.

We have observed a number of shared traits and common practices among the leaders who can foster the kind of culture change needed to help more students succeed. Together, these practices and associated beliefs amount to what we call "enlightened leadership," and they strongly resemble what is known in the literature as "transformational" and "adaptive" leadership (Bass & Riggio, 2006; Heifetz, 1994). In our experience, enlightened leaders balance a lofty vision with honest acknowledgment that realizing the vision will require hard work and difficult decisions. They listen as much as they talk—early, carefully, and often—to institutional practitioners at every level in a sincere effort to understand different experiences and points of view, even those of skeptics. They are not afraid to make tough decisions, but take the time to explain why and how they have made them—especially the unpopular ones. They create a culture of evidence, inquiry, and transparency by using data as a tool to inspire creativity and build a shared sense of responsibility for problems and solutions, and demonstrate support for shared goals through explicit, consistent, and relentless focus on student success. They sustain momentum and raise morale by keeping everyone's eyes on the big goals while guiding the incremental steps to them, and create small but meaningful incentives for innovation and collaboration. They foster shared commitment and pride by building on and formally recognizing successes, and encourage thoughtful risk taking. And last, but not least, they expect and accept failures as critical parts of the learning that amounts to a deep and durable commitment to responsible innovation on behalf of student success. One of the most important insights from the empirical research on leadership is that effective leaders serve as coaches instead of fixers—the best frontline managers operate as enablers, troubleshooters, resources, catalysts that make everyone else at all levels better problem solvers.

Pitfalls Around Data Translation and Use Abound.   Leaders at various levels must avoid unnecessary pitfalls around data use. Seemingly simple decisions, like how data are translated for various audiences, can have an enormous impact on how change efforts are viewed by key stakeholders. Treating data as though they speak for themselves or using data to shame rather than engage are key missteps that busy leaders can make as they seek to rally support for their efforts. The most skillful leaders we have seen are the ones who work hard to understand data and who learn how to use data as a tool to inspire creativity and build a shared sense of ownership for problems and solutions.

A cautionary tale: During the rollout of a national student success initiative, a senior administrator distributed the updated course completion

NEW DIRECTIONS FOR COMMUNITY COLLEGES • DOI: 10.1002/cc

numbers to each of the college's deans. Along with the data came a brief message that the student outcomes were not acceptable and that each department would be held accountable for increasing their pass rates. While some of the deans took advantage of the new data to explore them together with their chairs and faculty, one dean decided to gather the faculty in his department and shame them with the numbers. Telling the faculty that the situation had to change, he flipped through slide after slide of indecipherable charts and demanded that the faculty "commit to the completion agenda" in order to meet the goals set by a foundation-funded grant. After inevitable pushback from the faculty the dean improved his engagement approach over time, but his unproductive actions left many faculty disillusioned with all of the college's student success efforts.

A good model: One college president convened the college's entire full-time faculty in an auditorium to participate in a meeting with the college's institutional research staff. Faculty settled into their seats with their arms crossed, steeling themselves against what they expected to be a habitual finger-pointing exercise. Instead, the dean of institutional effectiveness distributed clickers to the faculty and asked for their assistance in exploring the college's data. The dean made it clear through her words and actions that she wasn't there to tell them what to do but instead to ask them "What should we do together?" The faculty began to participate, asking tough but substantive probing questions about the data and providing nuanced hypotheses about student outcomes of which no one was proud. After a number of these kinds of meetings, the faculty began to mobilize around the issue of student completion themselves, putting it at the top of their agenda for the coming year.

From Ideas to Action

By way of conclusion, we offer here two "checklists" of questions aimed at helping colleges assess both their culture of engagement and the climate around any proposed innovation. We view these checklists as diagnostic tools that can be used in a variety of ways including as focus group protocols; starting points for survey instruments; and discussion questions for meetings, planning sessions, and task forces. We encourage creative appropriation of these checklists, and suggest taking the time to consider how the answers to the questions may differ depending on one's role and perspective within the college. Adjunct faculty may answer questions very differently than their full-time peers, while professional advisors may have yet a different view from academic faculty altogether. Similarly, faculty may have different attitudes depending on their discipline or department. Using these questions to understand different stakeholder groups' perceptions of themselves and one another can be immensely helpful for identifying barriers to and opportunities for better collaborative problem solving on behalf of student success.

NEW DIRECTIONS FOR COMMUNITY COLLEGES • DOI: 10.1002/cc

Assessing the Institutional Culture of Engagement.

- What are the existing faculty engagement vehicles at our institution? Who "runs" them? Who participates?
- When are faculty and staff engaged in institutional interventions?
- How do college leaders communicate with adjunct faculty, full-time faculty, and student support staff?
- Are faculty and staff given public recognition for accomplishments? In what ways?
- To what extent do faculty and staff feel respected, heard, and valued by their departments and institutional leaders (even when those leaders make unpopular decisions)?
- Do faculty currently meet within their departments to discuss student success efforts?
- Do faculty currently meet with colleagues across departments to discuss student success efforts?
- Do faculty and staff meet regularly to discuss student success efforts?
- Around which types of initiatives or issues are adjunct and full-time faculty most likely to engage? How do we know this?
- Around which types of initiatives or issues are student support services staff most likely to engage? How do we know this?
- To what extent do faculty and staff interact around institutional data, and what do those interactions look and feel like?
- What kinds of professional development or colearning opportunities are available for faculty and staff?
- Who are the faculty champions of institutional student success efforts/initiatives?
- What are the barriers and challenges to meaningful engagement at our institution?
- What are the existing venues or opportunities into which more thoughtful engagement may be built?

Assessing Engagement With a Proposed Innovation.

- How have (or how will) faculty and staff come to learn about the existence of the innovation and gain a clear understanding of how it functions?
- How will this innovation "rate" when it comes to other top-tier concerns of faculty and staff?
- How have faculty and staff been involved in the development of the innovation?
- How will faculty and staff roles change as a result of the innovation? For whom may these changes be difficult and why?

- Do the faculty and staff who helped to develop the innovation believe that it is one that can make a difference in student completion and be scaled?
- How will faculty come to see that the chosen innovation is a good one, that it is important, and that it is important now?
- Which faculty and staff members do you most need to support and champion the change, and why?
- Who are the existing champions of the change or intervention?
- What actions can be taken to expand the number of faculty and staff champions of the intervention?
- What is the role of faculty and staff in the implementation? How much creative control are they given during implementation?
- What kind of conversations and deliberations do faculty and staff need to have in order to come to intellectual terms with the uncomfortable changes that may come with successful implementation of the innovation?
- What are the current conditions, supports, and incentives that either impede or support a sense of shared ownership for the innovation among faculty and staff?
- What kinds of conditions, supports, and incentives do faculty and staff need in order to accept and embrace the actual changes that come with adopting a new way of doing something?

We believe that the above questions can be used in any number of ways to help leaders at various levels within an institution better understand both opportunities for and barriers to the creation of a collaborative environment. While experience shows us that building the capacity of institutions to lead and execute effective engagement activities is essential to the long-term health of an institution, we also recognize that there are some issues that benefit from help from neutral outsiders. In the course of playing both roles (neutral outsider and capacity builder), we have learned that it is in leaders' best interests to decide when it might be important to bring in outside support and when it makes sense to tap internal actors to design and facilitate various engagement activities. There is no set recipe for success, or one-size-fits-all model, and context as well as resource constraints will determine much of what colleges can and will do. It is our hope that the lessons and checklists shared here will help faculty, staff, administrators, and leadership within colleges more thoughtfully navigate the complex and changing landscape on behalf of improved outcomes for students.

References

Bass, B., & Riggio, R. (2006). *Transformational leadership.* London, UK: Lawrence Erlbaum.

Brownson, R., Colditz, G., & Proctor, E. (2012, May). *Dissemination and implementation research in health: Translating science to practice.* New York, NY: Oxford University Press.

Edelman, L. B., Leachman, G., & McAdam, D. (2010). On law, organizations and social movements. *Annual Review of Law and Social Science, 6,* 653–685.

Ewell, P. T. (2008). Institutional characteristics and faculty/administrator perceptions of outcomes: An exploratory analysis. *Research in Higher Education, 30*(2), 113–136.

Gawande, A. (2009). *Checklist manifesto.* New York, NY: Metropolitan Books.

Heath, C., & Heath, D. (2010). *Switch: How to change things when change is hard.* New York, NY: Broadway Books.

Heifetz, R. A. (1994). *Leadership without easy answers.* Cambridge, MA: Harvard University Press.

Henderson, C., Dancy, M., & Niewiadomska-Bugaj, M. (2012). Use of research-based instructional strategies in introductory physics: Where do faculty leave the innovation-decision process? *Physical Review Special Topics Physics Education Research, 8*(2), 1–15. doi:10.1103/PhysRevSTPER.8.020104

Jex, M., & Britt, T. (2008). *Organizational psychology: A scientist-practitioner approach* (2nd ed.). Hoboken, NJ: Wiley.

Kellogg, K. C. (2012, March 12). *Not faking it: Making real change in response to regulation at two surgical teaching hospitals* (Working Paper). MIT Sloan School of Management.. Retrieved from http://www.researchgate.net/profile/Katherine _Kellogg/publication/229000550_NOT_FAKING_IT_MAKING_REAL_CHANGE_IN _RESPONSE_TO_REGULATION_AT_TWO_SURGICAL_TEACHING_HOSPITALS/file /60b7d52f0e091d515d.pdf

Kezar, A., & Sam, C. (2010). *Understanding the new majority of non-tenure-track faculty in higher education* [ASHE Higher Education Report, 36(4)]. San Francisco, CA: Jossey-Bass.

Klein, K. J., & Knight, A. P. (2005). Innovation implementation: Overcoming the challenge. *Current Directions in Psychological Science, 14*(5), 243–246. doi:10.1111/j.0963-7214.2005.00373.x

Kotter, J. (2011). Change management vs. change leadership—What's the difference? *Forbes.* Retrieved from http://www.forbes.com/sites/johnkotter/2011/07/12 /change-management-vs-change-leadership-whats-the-difference

Meyer, J., & Rowan, B. (1977). Institutionalized organizations: Formal structure as myth and ceremony. *American Journal of Sociology, 83,* 340–363.

Rogers, E. M. (2003). *Diffusion of innovations* (5th ed.). New York, NY: Free Press.

Shugart, S. M. (2012). The challenge to deep change: A brief cultural history of higher education. *Planning for Higher Education, 41*(2), 1–11. Retrieved from http://mojo .scup.org/forum/topics/the-challenge-to-deep-change-a-brief-cultural-history-of -higher

ALISON KADLEC *is a senior vice president at Public Agenda and directs public engagement programs and the Center for Advances in Public Engagement.*

ISAAC ROWLETT *is a senior public engagement associate in the Public Engagement Department at Public Agenda.*

9

This chapter summarizes the main lessons learned throughout the volume and highlights common needs with any large-scale reform along with common strategies.

Putting the Pieces Together: Lessons Learned for Future Reforms

Andrea Venezia, Katherine L. Hughes

As these chapters demonstrate, community colleges are experimenting with a wide range of practices that are intended to reach a large number of students and have a measurable impact on their progression through, and success in, college. The largest number of efforts profiled in this volume focuses on reforming developmental education, or on practices related to preparing students for college-level work. This is understandable given the college readiness crisis facing community colleges nationally and the seemingly intractable nature of traditional developmental education courses. The other pieces focus on tools, such as scaling, engaging colleagues, and using data. Those tools can be used in many different contexts on campus and the lessons are relatively transferable.

Key issues with any large reform process include:

- how to tweak an approach in one college, or take pieces from an approach to fit another context with a different student population;
- how much spread a reform can have and at what pace;
- how and when to know if the desired changes are occurring;
- scaling with the knowledge that there is rarely a one-size-fits-all model (e.g., adapting a model across an entire system); and
- sustaining the efforts and the changes after leaders/champions leave, and after targeted pots of funding are depleted.

It is tempting to try to transfer models intact from one setting to another, but it is clear throughout these chapters that much hinges on human elements such as personalities, relationships, and other interpersonal dynamics; leadership and politics; funding and resources, and priorities for

New Directions for Community Colleges, no. 167, Fall 2014 © 2014 Wiley Periodicals, Inc.
Published online in Wiley Online Library (wileyonlinelibrary.com) • DOI: 10.1002/cc.20114

those; and other factors that are not directly related to the content of a model.

Moreover, a theme consistently heard in the realm of technological applications in education is echoed throughout these chapters: *failures and setbacks are expected, acceptable, and shared.* In K–12 education, reforms are often so high-stakes and high-profile that it is difficult to share failures in ways that make it possible to learn from them. Higher education traditionally has a less reform-focused history, partially due to the relative independence it enjoys when compared with K–12. Not only are the efforts profiled here an indication of the flurry of reforms being undertaken in postsecondary currently, but several of them emerged within a climate in which not being perfect right out of the gate is accepted. As Kadlec and Rowlett state, "evidence from a range of fields suggests that most failures of innovation are in fact failures of implementation" (Chapter 8, p. 87). The successful reforms highlighted here have used an iterative process to learn and adjust during their implementation phases.

While they used different approaches, the reforms were similar not only in terms of many of their long-term goals and short-term objectives but also in terms of common strategies. These are described briefly next.

Use Data to Make the Case for Change, and for Formative Purposes and Course Corrections

Making data-driven decisions is a mantra throughout all levels of education right now, yet it is often unclear what this means in practice. Some institutions do not have analytical capacities and are almost entirely focused on responding to regulations and mandates, while others might have the capacity but not a culture that sees the value. Still others have traditional divides between academic and student affairs, which make it challenging not only to analyze data across campus functions but also to know where findings should be sent in order to have campus-wide actions developed.

Several of the chapters provide different lenses on this issue. From a framing perspective, Kadlec and Rowlett discuss the importance of translating data effectively for different audiences and engaging colleagues in making sense of data and determining follow-up actions. Hern and Snell learned in their work across California that reputable national research may not mobilize colleges to change; the response can sometimes be: *We don't have this problem at my college.* Rather, faculty need easy access to simple, relevant, actionable data points about their own students to understand where those students are stalled. As such, Bowling, Morrissey, and Fouts discuss how, in North Carolina, the college teams analyzed their own data, both qualitative and quantitative, to determine the factors associated with students not progressing successfully.

Adams and McKusick point out that data are also needed once new courses and pedagogies are piloted—such efforts must be carefully tracked

New Directions for Community Colleges • DOI: 10.1002/cc

and their continuation and expansion justified by visible effectiveness. They partnered with external researchers to continuously evaluate their reform efforts, as Montgomery County Community College is doing as well.

Thus, data inspire and undergird these reform efforts. But, as Rodwell shows, the accessible presentation of data can empower students as well. Rodwell makes the case that accessing information and data about degree pathways and their own progression through those pathways can be empowering for students in enabling them to make sense of complex options and navigate more productively.

Support From Leaders and Engagement of Faculty and Staff Is Key

As the chapter by Kadlec and Rowlett stresses, developing and implementing education reform is primarily a human endeavor—one that brings along with it all the benefits and challenges inherent in professional relationships and institutional politics. More specifically, leaders must be conscious of the "interplay between an institution's history, undergirding values, dominant dispositions, mission, and conditions in which its faculty, staff, and administrators operate" (Chapter 8, p. 88). These are not technical problems that lend themselves to off-the-shelf solutions.

Thus, we see at Miami Dade that the president determined the larger vision and pledged significant resources in support, but then allowed the college staff broadly to design, plan, and implement the work. There has been a strong emphasis on the cross-institutional teams communicating with one another. In Baltimore, Adams and McKusick emphasize how forming "a coalition of supporters from all areas of the college" (Chapter 2, p. 23) was necessary to bring about a reform to help "the whole learner" (Chapter 2, p. 23).

Provide Consistent, Clear, Transparent, and Structured Information for Students

This issue was addressed from several angles. Rodwell's chapter discussed the application of technology to provide essentially a pathways GPS system. Rodicio, Mayer, and Jenkins describe the overhaul of the intake process at Miami Dade College, including the significant resources invested with the understanding that helping students early on to understand their possible academic pathways and choose one to follow will improve completion.

Break Down Institutional Siloes

Collaboration between faculty and staff can be particularly effective in focusing on the entirety of students' experiences and not compartmentalizing academics and nonacademics separately. College leaders can set the tone for such cross-system collaborations. The Dadgar et al. chapter emphasizes the need for faculty and staff to work together to integrate coursework and supports. The perspective underlying that chapter is that the "separation of instruction and student supports may help colleges organize their services in more streamlined ways, but it can create obstacles for students if they do not know what kind of supports they need to access in order to succeed in their courses" (Chapter 4, p. 42). The changes at Miami Dade College exemplify the idea of partnership between student services and academic departments.

Professional Development Is Critically Important

With reforms comes the need for professional development, but these chapters show that it is not always immediately clear what that professional learning should look like, or how much is needed. The Accelerated Learning Program got off the ground with just a few hours of orientation and some informal support among the participating faculty members. As the program grew, administrators tried an online approach to professional learning, which did not last, and finally developed a successful five-day institute. At Montgomery County Community College, instructors newly teaching the *Concepts of Numbers* course were first provided with one-to-one orientation, which was soon seen as inadequate. The new course requires such significant shifts in teaching methods that a model was developed for small groups of participating instructors to meet regularly, supporting one another and providing input for ongoing course refinement.

Concluding Thoughts

When education reforms are fully implemented, the result must be a fundamentally different experience for students. While it is important for faculty, staff, and administrators to feel energized and passionate, real changes directly affect what students experience and how they experience it. These efforts should provide a greater sense of connection, coherence, transparency, support, and structure for students, in addition to improved educational opportunities. These strategies, especially when viewed as a whole, provide ways for colleges to combat the problems incurred by different personalities and contexts. Moreover, they maintain a focus on students—that the intent of these reforms is to provide opportunities for larger numbers of community college students to realize their dreams.

ANDREA VENEZIA *is an associate professor of public policy and administration and the executive director of the Institute for Higher Education Leadership & Policy at California State University, Sacramento.*

KATHERINE L. HUGHES *is the executive director of Community College and Higher Education Initiatives at the College Board.*

NEW DIRECTIONS FOR COMMUNITY COLLEGES • DOI: 10.1002/cc

INDEX

NEW DIRECTIONS FOR COMMUNITY COLLEGE

ORDER FORM SUBSCRIPTION AND SINGLE ISSUES

DISCOUNTED BACK ISSUES:

Use this form to receive 20% off all back issues of *New Directions for Community College*.
All single issues priced at **$23.20** (normally $29.00)

TITLE	ISSUE NO.	ISBN

Call 888-378-2537 or see mailing instructions below. When calling, mention the promotional code JBNND to receive your discount. For a complete list of issues, please visit www.josseybass.com/go/ndcc

SUBSCRIPTIONS: (1 YEAR, 4 ISSUES)

☐ New Order   ☐ Renewal

U.S.	☐ Individual: $89	☐ Institutional: $311
CANADA/MEXICO	☐ Individual: $89	☐ Institutional: $351
ALL OTHERS	☐ Individual: $113	☐ Institutional: $385

Call 888-378-2537 or see mailing and pricing instructions below.
Online subscriptions are available at www.onlinelibrary.wiley.com

ORDER TOTALS:

Issue / Subscription Amount: $ _____

Shipping Amount: $ _____
(for single issues only – subscription prices include shipping)

Total Amount: $ _____

SHIPPING CHARGES:	
First Item	$6.00
Each Add'l Item	$2.00

(No sales tax for U.S. subscriptions. Canadian residents, add GST for subscription orders. Individual rate subscriptions must be paid by personal check or credit card. Individual rate subscriptions may not be resold as library copies.)

BILLING & SHIPPING INFORMATION:

☐ **PAYMENT ENCLOSED:** *(U.S. check or money order only. All payments must be in U.S. dollars.)*

☐ **CREDIT CARD:**   ☐ VISA   ☐ MC   ☐ AMEX

Card number _____ Exp. Date_____

Card Holder Name_____ Card Issue # _____

Signature _____ Day Phone_____

☐ **BILL ME:** *(U.S. institutional orders only. Purchase order required.)*

Purchase order # _____
Federal Tax ID 13559302 • GST 89102-8052

Name_____

Address_____

Phone_____ E-mail_____

Copy or detach page and send to: **John Wiley & Sons, One Montgomery Street, Suite 1200, San Francisco, CA 94104-4594**

Order Form can also be faxed to: **888-481-2665**

PROMO JBNND

ARTHUR M. **COHEN**
FLORENCE B. **BRAWER**
CARRIE B. **KISKER**

COMPLETELY
REVISED
WITH
NEW TOPICS

THE

AMERICAN COMMUNITY COLLEGE

SIXTH EDITION

JB JOSSEY-BASS
A Wiley Brand

New
Sixth
Edition

THE AMERICAN COMMUNITY COLLEGE

COHEN
BRAWER
KISKER

For over thirty years, *The American Community College* has provided up-to-date information and statistics about community colleges. It has been widely used in graduate courses and by community college scholars, institutional researchers, and on-the-ground administrators.

The sixth edition has been significantly updated with discussions of current issues including:

- Outcomes and accountability
- The rise of for-profit colleges
- Leadership and administrative challenges
- Revenue generation
- Distance learning

The book concludes with a cogent response to contemporary criticisms of the institution.

JB JOSSEY-BASS™
A Wiley Brand